Agricultural Trade Policy

AEI STUDIES IN AGRICULTURAL POLICY

Agricultural Trade Policy
Letting Markets Work
Daniel A. Sumner

WITHDRAWN

The AEI Press

Publisher for the American Enterprise Institute

WASHINGTON, D.C.

1995

Available in the United States from the AEI Press, c/o Publisher Resources Inc., 1224 Heil Quaker Blvd., P.O. Box 7001, La Vergne, TN 37086-7001. Distributed outside the United States by arrangement with Eurospan, 3 Henrietta Street, London WC2E 8LU England.

Library of Congress Cataloging-in-Publication Data

Sumner, Daniel A.
    Agricultural trade policy: letting markets work / Daniel A. Sumner.
        p.   cm. — (AEI studies in agricultural policy)
    "A contribution to the American Enterprise Institute's project on agricultural policy reforms."
    Includes bibliographical references. (p.   ) and index.
    ISBN 0-8447-3910-3 (cloth : alk. paper). —ISBN 0-8447-3911-1 (paper : alk. paper)
    1. Tariff on farm produce—United States. 2. Produce trade—Government policy—United States. 3. Agriculture and state—United States. 4. Agricultural laws and legislation—United States. 5. Agriculture—United States—Finance. 6. Agriculture—Environmental aspects—United States. 7. General Agreement on Tariffs and Trade (Organization) 8. Canada. Treaties, etc. 1992 Oct. 7. 9. GATT. 10. NAFTA.   I. American Enterprise Institute for Public Policy Research   II. Title.   III. Series.
HF2651.F27U536   1995
382'.41'0973—dc20   95-31503
                                                                     CIP

1 3 5 7 9 10 8 6 4 2

The AEI Press
Publisher for the American Enterprise Institute
1150 17th Street, N.W., Washington, D.C.   20036

Printed in the United States of America

Contents

FIGURES

Foreword

Agricultural Trade Policy: Letting Markets Work, by Daniel A. Sumner, is one of eight in a series devoted to agricultural policy reform published by the American Enterprise Institute. AEI has a long tradition of contributing to the effort to understand and improve agricultural policy. AEI published books of essays before the 1977, 1981, and 1985 farm bills.

Agricultural policy has increasingly become part of the general policy debate. Whether the topic is trade, deregulation, or budget deficits, the same forces that affect other government programs are shaping farm policy discussions. It is fitting then for the AEI Studies in Agricultural Policy to deal with these issues with the same tools and approaches applied to other economic and social topics.

Periodic farm bills (along with budget acts) remain the principal vehicles for policy changes related to agriculture, food, and other rural issues. The 1990 farm legislation expires in 1995, and in recognition of the opportunity presented by the national debate surrounding the 1995 farm bill, the American Enterprise Institute has launched a major research project. The new farm bill will allow policy makers to bring agriculture more in line with market realities. The AEI studies were intended to capitalize on that important opportunity.

The AEI project includes studies on eight related topics prepared by recognized experts and scholars. Each study investigates the public rationale for government's role with respect to several agricultural issues. The authors have developed evidence on the effects of recent policies and analyzed alternatives. Most research was carried out in 1994, and draft reports were discussed at a policy research workshop held in Washington, D.C., November 3–4, 1994.

The individual topics include investigation of:

- the rationale for and consequences of farm programs in general
- specific reforms of current farm programs appropriate for 1995, including analysis of individual programs for grains, milk, cotton, and sugar, among others
- agricultural trade policy for commodities in the context of recent multilateral trade agreements, with attention both to long-run goals of free trade and to intermediate steps
- crop insurance and disaster aid policy
- the government's role in conservation of natural resources and the environmental consequences of farm programs
- farm credit policy, including analysis of both subsidy and regulation
- food safety policy
- the role of public R&D policy for agriculture, what parts of the research portfolio should be subsidized, and how the payoff to publicly supported science can be improved through better policy

Daniel A. Sumner, who directs the AEI project on agricultural policy, has prepared a superb analysis of current and prospective trade policy for agriculture, designed to help us move beyond the Uruguay Round agreement. He reviews how current trade policies are being modified by the recent trade agreeemnts and how recent policy and proposals have often been inconsistent with the stated aim of moving toward more open markets in world agriculture. Daniel discusses the limited benefits and large domestic costs of import protection. He shows that the rationales for export subsidies are either misapplied or out of date and therefore that the costs of the current policies far exceed their benefits. After considering the arguments for and consequences of import protection and export subsidy, the author argues that U.S. interests are better served by rapid and unilateral movement toward lower barriers for imports and the elimination of export subsidies.

Selected government policy may be helpful in allowing agriculture to become more efficient and effective. Unfortunately, most agricultural policy in the United States fails in that respect. In many ways, the policies of the past six decades have been counterproductive and counter to productivity. Now, in the final few years of the twentieth century, flaws in policies developed decades ago are finally becoming so obvious that farm policy observers and participants are willing to consider even eliminating many traditional subsidies and regulations. In the current context, another round of minor fixes is now seen as insufficient.

In 1995, Congress seems ready to ask tough questions about agricultural policy. How much reform is forthcoming, however, and which specific changes will be accomplished are not settled and depend on the information and analysis available to help guide the process. Understanding the consequences of alternative public policies is important. The AEI Studies in Agricultural Policy are designed to aid the process now and for the future by improving the knowledge base on which public policy is built.

CHRISTOPHER DEMUTH
American Enterprise Institute
for Public Policy Research

Acknowledgments

This book and the research underlying it have been much improved through the comments of several individuals. I wish to thank, in particular, Julian Alston, Colin Carter, Bruce Gardner, Roger Hitchner, D. Gale Johnson, Julius Katz, Hyunok Lee, Christine McCracken, Jeffrey McDonald, Andy Morton, David Orden, John Quilkey, Chirstopher Wolf, and the participants in a symposium held at the American Enterprise Institute in Washington, D.C., on November 3 and 4, 1994.

1
Introduction

For the past decade, much U.S. agricultural trade policy was a reaction to policies of protectionist importers and subsidized exporters, particularly the European Union. After more than a half-century of unapologetic protectionism and occasional export subsidies, the United States began to rationalize its trade barriers and renewed its export subsidies on the basis that similar policies were pursued elsewhere. The same rationalization was even invoked for domestic production subsidies and other income transfers to agriculture. Recognizing that exports were important to farm prosperity in the 1970s and that acreage reduction programs had limited effectiveness, however, the United States changed the mix of policies and programs. The new focus was on a combination of subsidized exports for selected commodities, domestic income supports, bilateral pressure to open markets, and multinational negotiations to reduce trade barriers and subsidies on a widespread basis. Residual and even expanded import protection for some commodities was pursued as well.

This seemingly contradictory mixture of programs and negotiating positions was pursued vigorously at the same time that annual land idling was moderated, domestic price floors were lowered, and government stocks were liquidated. Sometimes the United States did successfully use aggressive trade and domestic programs to pressure other nations to accept policies that they would not accept unilaterally. But in many cases the free trade negotiating position, with its accompanying rhetoric, was just a new excuse for the same import protection and subsidies that had always been favored by some domestic interests.

The North American Free Trade Agreement (NAFTA) and the multilateral Uruguay Round agreement of the General Agreement on Tariffs and Trade (GATT) have both finally become parts of the international trade environment. It is now possible to reevaluate U.S. agricultural trade programs without these major trade negotiations as a driving force for trade policy. This book pursues such an evaluation, with a focus both on reforms appropriate for the long-term and on reforms that may be possible to implement in the 1995 farm bill. The current policies, and the historical background of agricultural policies, are relevant for evaluating reforms and may have a determining role in what reforms prove feasible. This monograph, however, is not limited to considering alternatives likely to be pursued in 1995. As market conditions change, international rules are revised, and domestic political alignments adjust, new policies may become practical.

The approach taken here is conventional. The economic analysis is based on standard economic models, and the policy positions are familiar to most economists. Whereas there have been changes in the ensuing decades, many of the issues and much of the analysis are consistent with, for example, D. Gale Johnson's 1950 book *Trade and Agriculture: A Study of Inconsistent Policies.* That volume, written just after the GATT was created, analyzed such continuing U.S. policies as section 22 import quotas and subsidies for wheat exports. The present monograph is of more limited scope than *Trade and Agriculture,* and my domestic policy perspective more in tune with

Johnson's 1973 book *World Agriculture in Disarray*. This book is less concerned with finding trade policies that facilitate domestic subsidies and agricultural stabilization than was *Trade and Agriculture*. Instead I stress the problems caused by subverting a liberal trade policy to maintain outmoded farm subsidy programs.

Economists have been urging free trade for at least 200 years: nothing in the so-called new trade theory has changed the force of that basic prescription. (See, for example, Baldwin [1992] and Krugman [1987 and 1994].) Free trade should be easy to sell in U.S. agriculture, which has comparative advantage in many specific commodities. Further, as domestic farm programs have been reformed in the past decade, for example, to lower support prices, they are now more consistent with open markets than previously. The remaining policy inconsistencies are now mostly among trade policies themselves. The following chapters address a number of these policy problems.

Agricultural trade policy for the United States mainly consists of several specific export programs and a variety of import barriers. An alphabet soup of export subsidy programs includes the Export Enhancement Program (EEP), the Cottonseed Oil Assistance Program (COAP), the Sunflowerseed Oil Assistance Program (SOAP), and the Dairy Export Incentive Program (DEIP). The Market Promotion Program (MPP) and the Foreign Market Development Program (FMD) subsidize advertising and marketing efforts for exports. The GSM-102 and GSM-103 programs facilitate commercial export financing through credit guarantees. Finally, PL-480 and related programs operated by the Agency for International Development (AID) and the Department of Agriculture (USDA) provide free or low-cost food shipments.

Prior to the Uruguay Round agreement, agricultural imports were restricted by a variety of commodity specific quotas authorized under section 22 of the Agricultural Adjustment Act of 1933 (as amended) and the Meat Import Law. Implementation of the Uruguay Round agreement converts these barriers to GATT-bound tariff-rate quotas. A tariff-rate quota is essentially a set of two tariffs with the low duty rate applied for some guaranteed quantity of import access and a second, usually much higher, duty applied to provide protection above the "quota" amount. In addition to the preexisting tariffs and tariff-rate quotas, U.S. agricultural import policy includes several new trade barriers since the Uruguay Round agreement and NAFTA. In January 1994 a new domestic content law regulating the tobacco used in cigarettes was implemented to restrict tobacco imports. In July 1994 wheat imports from Canada were restricted through a "voluntary" bilateral agreement to create a new and "temporary" tariff-rate quota.

In addition to unilateral reform of the U.S. import and export programs, agricultural trade policy involves developing policy positions for continuing and upcoming international trade negotiations. The 1995 farm bill, for example, can contribute directly and indirectly to extending NAFTA to new nations. It will also set the parameters for continuing the multinational liberalization efforts in the World Trade Organization (WTO), the international agency created by the Uruguay Round agreement to supersede the GATT. Because the current tranche of export subsidy reductions and tariff cuts continues only through the end of the century, policies must be developed soon to determine how the reforms are to be continued. It took eight years to complete the Uruguay Round. If this timetable is indicative and if liberalization is to continue without interruption, then we are already late in starting the next round of multilateral trade negotiations.

The Food, Agriculture, Conservation and Trade Act of 1990 (FACT) included a number of provisions to guide the last years of the Uruguay Round negotiations. Besides implementing unilateral reforms, the 1995 farm bill can provide guidance and encourage an early start to continuing reforms that lead to freer agricultural trade on a global basis.

2

Common Rationalizations for Trade Barriers and Subsidies in Agriculture

The fundamental prescription of economists is open international markets. Trade barriers cause a nation to forgo gains from trade. Giving up those gains represents the substantial cost of trade barriers. Economists likewise presume that market forces provide appropriate signals and incentives for exports and that subsidized exports must be justified against this free trade ideal. The theory of gains from trade and of social losses from subsidy is well known but is reviewed below simply to put the argument on the table.

The two common classes of agricultural trade policies are protection from imports and subsidy of exports. At least in the United States, explicit export taxes or import subsidies are seldom applied. (But see Alston [1992] for a discussion of export restrictions and related domestic policies.) Import barriers and export subsidies are used often in agriculture, and often both are used for the same commodity. Trade policies to deviate from open unsubsidized trade in agriculture are frequently justified on grounds similar to those used for domestic farm subsidies. The idea that U.S. agricultural industries need a subsidy or protection because incomes or rates of return are low or because markets are extremely variable is still presented, although it has lost considerable favor in recent years. Sometimes farm export subsidies are rationalized as supplements to domestic subsidies, and sometimes trade barriers are used as substitutes for direct domestic subsidies. Trade policies are sometimes rationalized as necessary to mitigate some effects of domestic programs. But more often trade barriers for farm commodities are used to protect the domestic subsidy programs themselves. In that case the trade policy is justified simply as a tool to help make the domestic subsidy effective, and the more fundamental public policy rationale is reserved for the domestic program. Therefore, as is true for domestic programs, agricultural trade policies vary by commodity and change over time.

This chapter is not devoted to understanding why, in a political economy sense, particular polices are chosen. Rather, the chapter attempts the more modest task of listing some frequent reasons to justify trade interventions. The politics behind trade barriers and subsidies may be closely related to the stated public policy rationale, or the issue may be a more simple function of income redistribution and political influence. Those who wish to see more on the economics of agricultural politics in the context of trade policy, a popular topic for research, are encouraged to consult, for example, Gardner (1983 and 1994), Orden (1994), and Alston, Carter, and Smith (1993).

Gains from Trade

International trade arises for the same reasons that domestic exchange occurs: a resource, good, or service is more valuable to the buyer than to the seller. If a New Jersey pasta maker finds it profitable to pay $150 per ton for durum wheat, and the Canadian Wheat Board is willing to sell at that price, both sides evidently gain. The U.S. national income improves because the pasta maker is better off, and Canadian national income improves because the Canadian grain industry is better off. If U.S. policy is devoted to the welfare of U.S. residents, then only the well-being of the pasta firm (and others in the U.S.) is of interest here, and the benefit of trade to foreigners is ignored. If the welfare of foreigners is also important, gains from trade on both sides of the border should be considered, and if foreigners are given equal weight in the welfare calculation, there is no difference between international trade and trade within a nation.

International trade may be thought to benefit domestic interests only half as much as gains from trade within the nation. An exporting nation gains from selling more at a higher price, and an importer gains from buying more at a lower price. Blocking the transaction would be costly to both. But blocking the transactions of willing buyers and sellers within a nation costs that nation on both sides of the transaction. This may be one reason that creating barriers on international trade may seem easier than creating barriers within a nation. For other reasons, dealing with differences in factor endowments, trade between geographically diverse nations (particularly in agriculture) may carry larger benefits to each party than does domestic trade.

International trade occurs when prices between nations diverge. Such divergence may have a number of underlying causes, but the observation of price differences is enough to suggest the potential for trade. Trading itself has costs (for transportation and other features of the transaction) such that the price difference must be large enough to overcome the cost of the transaction. The larger the costs of a transaction, the more prices must differ before trade is profitable.

Countries (and individuals) tend to sell more of what they are relatively good at producing. An econometrician who types 120 words a minute but bills $200 per hour for econometric analysis may hire someone to type reports. It is obviously more profitable to do econometrics and pay $20 per hour to someone who types only half as fast. Absolute productivity is not the key factor in determining trade; relative productivity and relative prices matter. Following a similar logic, California imports substantial amounts of wheat and feed grains and uses the Central Valley mainly to grow fruits and vegetables.

Gains from trade also occur as a result of economies of scale and dynamic gains from specialization. Exchange allows a nation (or a firm or an individual) to focus its attention toward activities for which it has some particular expertise relative to other nations. If economies of scale in production exist over the relevant range, the economy that specializes will produce at a lower cost than the economy that has no access to imports and therefore produces a wider variety of goods and services at home. Improved opportunities to exploit economies of scale are particularly important for small domestic industries that do not enjoy a sufficiently large local demand. In those cases access to exports allows the use of lower-cost production processes. Likewise, importing may allow consumers of final goods or inputs to have access to lower-cost goods and services produced in the exporting nation that may (because of the export market) take advantage of economies of scale. Specialization may also allow faster improvements of productivity, and thus increase benefits over time. "Learning-by-doing" is one of the phrases used to describe the process by which costs are lowered as production takes place. Further, more specialization brings increased investments in knowledge and improved productivity.

Finally, in commodity markets it has become well established that more open borders reduce the price variability in world markets (Johnson 1975; Tyers and Anderson 1992). World market price variability has often been cited as a reason for agricultural trade policies. Countries claim that they restrict imports and subsidize exports to maintain policies better to assure domestic consumers and producers stable prices. The observed variability in world markets, however, is in part determined by trade policies. Most price variability in agriculture has at its core yield fluctuations caused by weather. The more restricted is the market, the lower the relevant elasticity of demand and the more prices are affected. The broader the market over which any given yield shock is spread, the less price variability is created.

Import Barriers

Against this background of general gains from trade are a limited number of situations in which import barriers could theoretically improve the national well-being. Many arguments have been used to block imports, but these arguments are often based on nothing more than economic misunderstanding coupled with the recognition that some local interests always benefit from import barriers. The following arguments have some claim to theoretical legitimacy or at least to a historical pedigree (see Vousden [1990] or Krishna and Thursby [1990]; for an agricultural context, see Houck [1986]):

- to provide revenue
- to provide national food security or security of strategic resources
- to protect new industries with potential growth
- to improve international purchase prices
- to protect plant, animal, and human health
- to counteract trade policies and domestic subsidies of other nations
- to limit interference with domestic subsidy programs
- to reduce costs of adjustment for domestic industries
- to respond to imperfect competition in international markets

- to respond strategically to encourage multilateral trade liberalization

Each of these arguments has been presented to justify import barriers on grounds other than the simple fact that some domestic interest would prefer not to compete with imports.

Revenue. Historically taxes on imports or even exports were a significant source of revenue for governments. Currently import tariffs are a trivial revenue source for the U.S. government, which has developed an ability to tax its residents with fiendish effectiveness. But tariff revenue became an issuein the debate over the implementation of the Uruguay Round agreement. Under recent congressional budget rules, new revenue sources or reduced spending was required as a part of the implementation legislation. Although the tariff revenue at stake was trivial compared with the size of the U.S. government budget (not more than $2.5 billion per year out of a federal budget of $1,500 billion), nonetheless the issue became contentious.

Security. A traditional argument of food importers has been that, as a matter of national food security, it is dangerous to rely on imports for food. Protection of a limited production capacity for strategic materials or vital goods may make sense, as may investing in the security of import sources. Much more common, however, is the use of "security" to rationalize import barriers for more mundane reasons. Japan, for example, rationalized its absolute ban on rice imports partly on food security grounds even though rice is produced with imported petroleum, most other foods are already imported, a significant amount of rice is used for rice wine or other nonvital demands, and (as their 1993 experience showed) banning imports altogether creates vulnerability to local weather. In the United States, food security is not used to justify trade barriers. Lack of plausibility was likely not the only reason for such forbearance. National security, for example, was used until 1993 as an official rationale for large subsidies for sheep production.

Infant Industries. A traditional argument for import protection is to help a small local industry get started in a protected environment free from competition from mature low-cost foreign firms. The plausibility of the infant industry argument for import protection in most real situations is weak. If a domestic industry's cost disadvantage is truly temporary, it would be profitable for the industry interest to produce at a loss in the short run and to recoup the losses later when its costs are lower. Further, once protection is in place, it is difficult to remove it. Successful industries become particularly adept at keeping protection in place as they mature and have potential profits at risk.

Whatever its potential plausibility, the infant industry argument is not used in any widespread way to rationalize import barriers for U.S. agriculture. The industries that are most protected from imports (dairy, beef, peanuts, sugar, and wheat) tend to be mature and large. Import barriers for these industries are based on other rationales.

Monopsony Power. Large countries may be able to use limits on imports to lower the import price facing the nation. When a single nation makes up a significant part of the market for a particular commodity, an import tariff or quota can be profitable for the nation as a whole, if its application results in a lower net import price. The United States may have monopsony power in some agricultural markets, particularly for beef, sugar, some cheese, and tropical fruits and beverages. For beef, sugar, and cheese, the United States typically allowed foreign firms to capture the import quota rents; for the tropical commodities, the United States does not use import barriers. In the next section, dealing with export policy, the use of monopoly power in export markets is seen as a more important factor in U.S. trade policy for agriculture.

Sanitary and Phytosanitary Barriers. In agricultural markets it is common to use import barriers to protect against animal and plant diseases. Such sanitary and phytosanitary trade restrictions are simply extensions of domestic rules that limit the movement of plants or animal products that may cause widespread disease concerns. An analogous reason for import restrictions is based on human health concerns. In this case, if there are restrictions on sales in the domestic market based on pesticide residues, the same rules would be expected to apply to imports.

Import Barriers to Counteract Exporters' Subsidies. A well-established tradition in trade law and practice is that nations use import tariffs to respond either to explicit export subsidies or to exports below domestic prices or costs of production. International rules for countervailing duties and antidumping measures, for example, have been included in the General Agreement on Tariffs and Trade since its inception. Although it is accepted in international trade law, it is not obvious that countervailing trade duties or other import barriers to counteract subsidized exports improve national well-being. When an exporter provides a product at low prices, consumers gain. It matters little whether the observed import price is based on subsidies or low costs of production. Gains from trade depend only on the ability to acquire the product at a price below that offered by domestic competition.

A different argument would be to guard against the use of export subsidies as a strategy to cause competitors to leave the industry. Then, if there are fixed costs of reentry, the foreign firms may capture monopoly rents in the long run when the export subsidies are removed. Such a strategic policy is never applied and is not a reasonable justification for protection.

Limiting Interference with Domestic Policies. If a domestic program is accepted as in the national interest, then it may be considered an extension of that national interest to establish trade polices that protect the domestic program. U.S. law codified this reasoning for trade barriers in section 22 of the Agricultural Adjustment Act of 1933. Though amended several times, section 22 remains the legal basis for most of the nontariff trade barriers used by U.S. agricultural interests. Section 22 states simply that a tariff or nontariff protection may be applied any time imports are expected to interfere materially with the operation of the farm program for some commodity.

As a matter of economic policy, the domestic program rationale for trade barriers is based on two premises. First, the underlying farm program must be justified, and, second, the program must truly require a trade barrier for its operation. It is often difficult to find convincing economic reasoning to support domestic farm programs, and this is particularly true for the types of programs that require trade barriers for their successful implementation. Further, most policy objectives can be achieved without resorting to import restraints.

Another related but distinct argument may be more relevant to understanding the role of trade barriers in the context of domestic programs. If the domestic program is considered immutable, the economic rationale of the trade policy must be considered in light of the domestic program. In this case, even if there is no convincing rationale for the domestic program, the trade barrier could reduce the national income losses attributable to the domestic program. The more appropriate policy is to remove the domestic program, rather than to add a trade barrier.

Imperfect Competition and International Trade Policy.

14

Arguments used to justify government intervention in imperfectly competitive domestic markets suggest the potential for trade policies to take advantage of oligopolistic market forces in trade. Nations may engage in strategic import barriers to help individual firms compete in international trade against the strategic behavior of other firms or nations (Krishna and Thursby [1990] survey the literature in an agricultural context). This idea seems to have little applicability in agriculture.

Strategic Policy to Encourage Liberalization. During negotiation a country may maintain trade barriers to encourage the multilateral movement to liberalization. This argument accepts that lower trade barriers are the ultimate objective but notes that multilateral liberalization is preferred to unilateral liberalization. The agreement to remove a nation's barriers may be used as an incentive for a trading partner to remove its barriers. As with some of the rationales listed above, this argument may apply in the short run but is not an argument for permanent maintenance of import restrictions.

Adjustment Costs. The adjustment-cost argument is usually made to justify maintaining existing trade barriers, not creating barriers. If current patterns of investment were based on import protection, removing that protection would entail costs of adjustment. Thus, even if the initial barriers could not be justified on grounds of national welfare, there could be grounds for reducing barriers gradually to reduce losses from investments already made. As with many economic policy changes, trade barriers tend to be reduced gradually in practice.

Export Subsidies

Many economic rationalizations used for export programs are analogous to those used for import barriers. Explicit export taxes or quotas may lower domestic prices or provide government revenue. Although they are used in some less developed countries, they are not used with any regularity by the United States; thus this section does not discuss export barriers. The U.S. use of export embargoes to selected markets has been a part of international political or defense policy, and embargoes will not be analyzed here. (USDA [1986] provides a comprehensive examination of U.S. agricultural embargoes, as in Abbott and Paarlberg [1986].)

Some rationalizations for export subsidies that are less important or obviously parallel to those listed in the previous section will not be repeated here. We are left with the following list:

- to offset some of the effects of domestic farm programs
- to respond to opportunities of increasing returns to scale and imperfect competition
- to exploit international market power
- to react to the trade policies of other countries
- to respond to the trade policies of other countries so as to encourage multilateral liberalization

Offsetting Costs of Domestic Farm Programs. A class of second-best arguments applies under which an export subsidy offsets some of the costs of another policy or distortion. If the other policy itself is costly, the better idea may be simply to eliminate it. If, however, a domestic income transfer to farmers is considered appropriate for some reason, or the policy or distortion is simply not open for modification, then it could be sensible to apply an export subsidy to reduce the costs of the original policy. The validity of second-best arguments depends on the specifics of each case. We will examine a specific variant of this rationale when we consider the Export Enhancement Program.

Increasing Returns to Scale and International Monopoly Rents. With increasing returns, some gains from trade are based on exports increasing the scale of operation and thus lowering costs of production. Even if factor endowments and technologies are identical in two countries, the world may be better off with one country producing all the wheat and another all the milk if economies of scale imply that both wheat and milk are cheaper as a result.

The implication for trade policy is that with imperfect competition some government subsidy could be used to allow a domestic industry rather than a foreign industry to gain the economic monopoly rents from producing in a world market with few firms. The simplest story is one in which only one or a few firms operate in a world market because economies of scale are so important. In this case a strategic subsidy can allow a domestic firm to remain in the market while foreign firms either exit or do not enter. Then the excess economic profits go to the domestic economy.

This is a theoretic argument for strategic subsidization, not for any particular trade policies. Further, when the argument is elaborated with specifics about how firms and governments can react to each other's policies or declarations, the argument can be one of export subsidies, taxes, import quotas, or tariffs as well as direct production subsidies.

The relevance of this strategic trade policy argument to agriculture seems questionable at best. Indeed one of its developers recently stressed the inapplicability of the new trade theory to agriculture as follows: "The ability to grow wheat cheaply depends on soil ... in other words comparative advantage is still alive and well, and still governs much of trade. On the other hand not every industry is like wheat" (Krugman 1994).

Wheat production involves many farms; comparative advantage, rather than scale economies and imperfect competition, is surely a major factor in agricultural commodity trade. It is also true, however, that agricultural trade in bulk commodities (as with wheat) and agricultural manufacturing (as with cigarettes) often involves relatively few firms. In these cases, monopoly rents may occur to some degree. The idea of trade policy for agriculture based on imperfect competition should not be dismissed out of hand. Rather, it should be dismissed after due consideration.

Export Market Power. Normally a country with export market power would tax or otherwise limit exports. See, for example, Alston (1992), who discusses the potential for export cartels in agricultural industries. It may seem, then, that this rationale could not apply to export subsidy policy. In the context of a fixed policy that taxed production or otherwise limited output (say by a production quota or land set-aside), however, an export subsidy applied selectively could increase national welfare by applying (implicitly) a differential export tax. This is not the first policy choice in such a situation.

Reactions to Other Countries' Trade Policies. A common rationale for export subsidies is to compete with an export subsidy used by other exporters. If the competitors' export subsidy is considered immutable, however, it is hard to see how national welfare is improved by supplying foreign consumers with a subsidy. It may seem unfair to producers that they must compete against a foreign government as well as a foreign industry, but that in itself is not a convincing argument for subsidy. As in other cases, however, if there are fixed reentry costs or other similar sorts of adjustment costs and if the foreign subsidies are temporary, it may make sense to use temporary subsidies to maintain access to the market. A nation may provide a subsidy in this case if the fixed reentry costs apply to the nation and if the gains apply to all national firms. A tax on the firms involved seems appropriate to finance the policy.

This argument for temporary subsidies could also apply when other countries are likely to institute import restraints that allocate access to markets based on historical exports. In this case it could be reasonable to subsidize temporarily to increase a nation's share of the forthcoming quota.

Encourage Multilateral Liberalization. It may seem ironic that one of the more compelling arguments in favor of trade distortions is to eliminate distortions. This argument applies where export subsidies used by one country increase the costs for other countries' export subsidies and other distorting trade policies. Just as military expenditures can be justified on the basis of encouraging disarmament, export subsidies could in principle create incentives for a group of countries to undertake reforms jointly. In particular, if by driving down world prices, export subsidy costs are increased for one's competitors, the result is an added incentive for multilateral trade disarmament.

Implications

The list of rationalizations for trade barriers and subsidies listed here is not meant as an endorsement for protectionist policies. The applicability of the rationales listed is quite limited, and few policies are justified on these grounds. The purpose of this chapter is to list the potential arguments and to highlight just how limited their applicability is.

The following chapters describe actual agricultural trade policies and show that in actual cases no compelling national interest is served by agricultural trade subsidy and protection. The issue becomes how best to reform agricultural trade policy along with the other policies that distort our economic relationships.

3

Recent Agricultural Trade Patterns and Trade Agreements

This chapter provides some of the descriptive background necessary for an evaluation of U.S. agricultural trade policies and programs. The first topic in such a background is a brief history of U.S. agricultural trade in recent decades and a description of the current trade patterns. This information leads to the conclusion that international trade is indeed important to U.S. agriculture and that agricultural trade is important to the U.S. economy.

Following the discussion of trade patterns is a review of the North American Free Trade Agreement. Next I discuss the Uruguay Round multilateral trade agreement that was negotiated to reform the General Agreement on Tariffs and Trade and created the World Trade Organization. The two agreements provide both new constraints and new opportunities for U.S. agricultural trade policy. The description of each agreement is accompanied by a brief summary of the major trade impacts anticipated.

Recent Agricultural Trade Patterns

The United States was a major agricultural trading nation early in its history and for many years thereafter.

The nation subsequently went through a long period of a more inward orientation in agriculture. We now take for granted that the United States is a net exporter of agricultural products. This was not the case, however, in the middle part of this century. Except for the years during and immediately after World War II, the United States was a minor exporter of agricultural goods and generally imported more than it exported. The value of U.S. agricultural exports, for example, exceeded the value of imports for only two years of the decade of the 1950s.

In 1954, for example, U.S. exports were valued at $3.1 billion, and agricultural imports were $4.0 billion. To get a sense of their importance, these figures may be compared to gross farm revenue of $34.2 billion for that year. In 1994, agricultural exports were projected to total $43.5 billion, compared with imports of $25.5 billion and gross farm revenue of approximately $210 billion. Thus, in the past forty years, farm exports have gone from less than one-tenth the size of gross farm revenue to more than one-fifth the size of gross revenue. This increased export orientation was accompanied by import growth as well. The agricultural economy was becoming more international in general.

Table 3–1 shows that the growth of agricultural trade has not been constant. Imports actually declined in the 1950s. They expanded rapidly in nominal terms in the 1970s but did not keep up with the rapid expansion in agricultural exports. During the 1980s, while U.S. agricultural exports declined and then gradually approached the prior level, imports continued to expand. In general, agricultural imports tend to grow along with the size of the national income.

U.S. agricultural exports grew gradually until the early 1970s, when they expanded at an unprecedented pace. Exports reached a peak in 1981 that is exceeded in nominal terms only by current projections for 1995. But at more than 25 percent of total gross farm revenue for the year, 1981 exports were a more important source of

TABLE 3–1

U.S. Exports and Imports of Agricultural Commodities,
1941–1995
(billions of dollars)

Year [a]	Total Exports	Total Imports	Agricultural Trade Balance
1941	0.7	1.7	-1.0
1951	4.0	5.2	-1.1
1961	5.0	3.7	1.3
1971	7.7	5.8	1.9
1981	43.4	16.8	26.6
1993	42.5	24.5	18.0
1994	43.5	26.4	17.1
1995 (forecast) 45.0		28.0	17.0

a. Calendar years for 1941–1971, fiscal years for 1981–1995.
Sources: U.S. President's Council of Economic Advisers, *Economic Report of the President* (Washington, D.C.: GPO, 1993); U.S. Department of Agriculture, Economic Research Service, *Agricultural Outlook,* May 1995, and *Agricultural Export Situation and Outlook,* November 29, 1994.

demand than will be exports in 1995, even if current projections are realized. The rapid growth in U.S. agricultural exports in the 1970s was led by the grains and oilseed industries, which were not important sources of exports in earlier years. In contrast, the recent period of export growth since 1987 has been led by horticultural products and meats.

Agriculture has long played an important role in the total export picture of the United States. U.S. total exports, for example, were so small that farm exports even in 1965 were almost 24 percent of total merchandise exports. By 1971, agriculture's share had declined to 18 percent of the total, but it grew to 25 percent in 1974, before it declined gradually and unevenly over the next twenty years. Agricultural products represent a still sizable 10 percent of the total value of merchandise exports of the United States. This compares with a share of gross domestic product of about 2 percent. Given the importance of services in the domestic economy, unsurprisingly agriculture makes up a larger share of merchandise exports than of the gross domestic product. Further, the increasing share of processed and semiprocessed goods in agricultural exports means that exports classified as agricultural include more value that is added after the commodity leaves the farm, and thus agricultural exports and manufactured exports are becoming less distinct.

Table 3–2 describes the current pattern of exports and imports across commodities. Almost half of all U.S. agricultural exports is still comprised of whole or processed grains and oilseeds. Meat and poultry exports have grown to about 10 percent of total exports. Fruits, nuts, and vegetables were about 16 percent of total exports in 1993 and are projected by the U.S. Department of Agriculture to be almost 20 percent of total agricultural exports in fiscal year 1995.

Agricultural imports are often categorized as those that are competitive with U.S. agricultural production and those that are not. Noncompetitive imports are made up of coffee, tea, cocoa, bananas, spices, rubber, raw silk, and such products. These have recently constituted about 25 percent of all agricultural imports.

This review of recent trade patterns documents two key facts. First, agricultural trade is important. Exports are an important part of total demand for agricultural production in the United States, and imports are an important part of the supply of food and fiber in the United States. Second, the United States exports and imports a wide variety of products. Exports are not dominated by grains and oilseeds, and imports are not dominated by sugar, peanuts, and dairy products even though these commodities dominate the policy discussions.

TABLE 3–2: U.S. AGRICULTURAL EXPORTS AND IMPORTS BY COMMODITY, FISCAL 1993

	Agricultural Exports			Agricultural Imports	
Product	%	$ (millions)	Product	%	$ (millions)
Meats, preparations from meats excluding poultry meats	7.9	3,349	Meats, preparations from meats excluding poultry meats	11.1	2,726
Poultry meats	2.4	1,031	Poultry meats	0.6	137
Dairy products	1.8	762	Dairy products	3.5	860
Live animals	0.8	358	Animals live	6.4	1,569
All other animals	6.0	2,927	All other animals	1.6	384
Feed grains	12.4	5,261	Grains, feeds	6.7	1,639
Feeds, other grains	7.3	3,123			
Wheat and flour	11.7	4,954	Bananas	4.4	1,083
Rice	1.8	766	Other fruits, nuts, preparations excluding juices	7.8	1,905
Fruits, nuts, preparations	9.0	3,832	Vegetables	10.0	2,440
Vegetables, preparations	7.6	3,220	Tobacco	4.5	1,101
Tobacco (unmanufactured)	3.4	1,443	Sugar	2.4	591
Sugar	0.2	106	Coffee, tea	12.3	3,018
Seeds	1.5	648	Cotton	0.0	11
Cotton	3.6	1,526	Oilseeds, products	4.9	1,204
Oilseeds, products	16.9	7,211	Other	25.7	6,279
Other	8.1	3,434	Total	100	24,450
Total	100	42,590			

SOURCE: United States Department of Agriculture, Economic Research Service, *Agricultural Outlook*, November 1994.

Besides documenting the importance of trade to current agricultural supply and demand, recent data and current trends suggest that trade has the potential to become even more important. Statements about the increasing share of world population and income outside the United States have become so commonplace that they may seem rhetorical. Economic growth, especially in Asia and Latin America, means there is the potential for expanding exports as long as market access is available. Further, if access can be improved, even regions with relatively static demands for food and fiber can provide new markets for trade.

Current trade patterns make clear that agricultural trade policy is significant for the agricultural economy. This significance is reinforced by the potential for the growth in agricultural trade, particularly if trade policies are reformed. Simply expanding the value of exports and imports is not an end in itself.

Trade is valuable when it contributes to the strength of the total economy. The mercantilist logic (or illogic) that encourages some to think that imports are bad for the economy also causes some to infer mistakenly that more exports are good for the economy no matter what the source. The importance of trade itself to the U.S. agricultural economy should not be misinterpreted or overstated. Domestic markets and domestic consumers matter too, and using higher taxes or higher domestic consumer prices to "buy" more exports does not contribute to the health of the economy. The slogan "export good–import bad" simply makes no economic sense.

Agricultural trade policy in the United States takes place within the context of international market conditions, trade policies of customers and competitors, and multilateral trading rules. The Uruguay Round of the GATT agreement and NAFTA affect each of these items, and future adjustments to U.S. trade policy must be considered in the context of these trade agreements.

The North American Free Trade Agreement

Implementation of NAFTA began in January 1994 with tariff cuts and other related changes in trading rules between the United States and Mexico and between Mexico and Canada. The agricultural tariff cuts and other measures of the Canada–United States Trade Agreement (CUSTA) of 1989 continue to be implemented gradually. NAFTA did little to modify that agreement and is not a "free trade" agreement between the United States and Canada.

The Effects of NAFTA on Policy and Programs. NAFTA is leading to an open border between the United States and Mexico. Nontariff barriers were converted to tariffs, and all agricultural tariffs, including the newly created ones, are being gradually reduced to zero. Many tariffs were removed on January 1, 1994; others are to be eliminated in five years, and some, in ten years. For commodities of particular political or economic sensitivity on each side of the border, liberalization is subject to long implementation periods with provisions for quantitative controls during the interim period. In Mexico, for example, a gradually expanding import quota for corn is supplemented by high and initially prohibitive overquota tariffs that will gradually decline to zero by the year 2007. In the United States, tariff reductions for frozen concentrated orange juice and a few other products will be quite slow: free trade will not be completed for fifteen years. But between the United States and Mexico the agreement will ultimately lead to free trade in agriculture (USDA 1993).

Domestic farm programs are not directly affected by NAFTA, but to the extent that a program depends on sealing the border, it faces modifications. In the United States such modifications have been minor at most. In Mexico some changes have been significant. The high price-support policy for corn in Mexico, for example, was changed to a policy of decoupled direct payments and planting flexibility.

Export programs such as the Export Enhancement Program or the Market Promotion Program are unaffected by NAFTA. These programs, however, may be subject to countervailing duties, and any limits imposed by the Uruguay Round agreement apply as well.

The Effects of NAFTA on Agricultural Trade. Initial evidence is that NAFTA has accounted for increased imports and exports of agricultural goods between the United States and Mexico. With horticultural trade, for example, Mexico has increased fresh tomato and other fruit and vegetable exports to the United States, and the United States has shipped more apples, pears, and grapes to Mexico in response to removal of import restrictions and lower tariff barriers (USDA 1994c). Projections of trade consequences made in 1993 still seem applicable (USDA 1993). In general the most important trade consequences of NAFTA depend on the economic growth prospects in Mexico, and that is obviously a long-term affair.

A couple of specific examples provide a flavor of what NAFTA means for major U.S. agricultural industries. For wheat, NAFTA eliminated the Mexican import licensing system and substituted a 15 percent ad valorem tariff, which will be reduced to zero over ten years. Given that export programs and the deficiency payment programs are not affected directly, the significant consequence for the U.S. wheat industry is better and more assured access to the Mexican market. In the past, exports to Mexico have been quite variable, ranging from 50,000 tons to more than 1 million tons per year. Mexico is a significant market for wheat, but even when U.S. exports to Mexico remain consistently in the range of 1.2 to 1.3 million tons, this accounts for only about 2 percent of U.S. production or 4 percent of exports.

Beef trade impacts may be somewhat more significant but still moderate at best. The beef industries in the United States and Mexico have worked together for many years. Mexico supplies cattle to feedlots in the Southwest, and some slaughter cattle and beef are shipped to Mexico. Relatively minor trade barriers for the beef and cattle trade existed recently until Mexico imposed new tariffs in November 1992 of 15 percent for live cattle, 20 percent for fresh beef, and 25 percent for frozen beef. These tariffs were eliminated by NAFTA for the United States and Canada but are unaffected by NAFTA for other suppliers. NAFTA also eliminated the U.S. meat import law restriction on imports from Mexico and will gradually eliminate the two cents per pound tariff. Neither of these changes is expected to have measurable impacts on beef imports.

USDA projected that NAFTA would improve cattle and beef prices by about 1 percent and raise revenues for the cattle industry by some $400 million or slightly more than 1 percent (USDA 1993). Among the most important consequences for the beef industry is the assurance that Mexico cannot reverse course again and raise barriers that it had previously lowered. The direct revenue gains to the beef industry are small, and even these are tempered by expected marginal increases in feed grain prices.

The Uruguay Round Agreement on Agriculture

The Uruguay Round GATT agreement was many years in coming. The negotiations were formally launched in 1986 (after several years of preliminary discussions), and implementation begins in 1995. Agricultural tariff cuts and other policy changes are to be phased in over a six-year period in the developed countries and over a ten-year period for developing countries. From the beginning of the negotiation to the completion of the required policy changes, the Uruguay Round will have consumed more than two decades. It is no wonder then why many observers and participants became impatient, and why some continue to question whether the results (or anticipated results) have been worth the effort (McCalla 1993; Rossen et al. 1994; Sanderson n.d.).

Developing countries are given special treatment under the agreement. Besides slower implementation they were required to make smaller reduction commitments, equal to two-thirds of the corresponding commitment for developed countries. Least-developed countries are exempt from reduction commitments. Since the least developed countries are mostly insignificant in world commercial trade, this last exception will have only a marginal impact on world agriculture.

The changes in trade policy set out in the Uruguay Round agreement apply to all countries that ratify the agreement and join the World Trade Organization. Further, if a country is not a member, the benefits of improved access to markets do not apply to exports from that country. The major countries not yet members of the WTO are China, Taiwan, and Russia (and other nations that were part of the former Soviet bloc). Each of these countries, however, has applied for membership and is likely to join in the near future.

The agreement contains multiple chapters, many of which bear on agricultural trade and policy. This section, however, is focused primarily on the agricultural agreement itself. (See also International Agricultural Trade Research Consortium [1994] and USDA [1994a, b].) The agreement provisions dealing with sanitary and phytosanitary measures and food safety are discussed first. Then the provisions related to border barriers, export subsidies, and internal supports are outlined.

Sanitary and Phytosanitary Measures in the Uruguay Round. The Uruguay Round agreement requires that trade restrictions that claim to be based on threats to human, animal, or plant health and safety be scientifically grounded. Negotiations on the sanitary and phytosanitary rules were essentially completed early in 1992, when major trading nations agreed on the final language. In particular it was agreed at that time that social factors and public opinion would not be considered legitimate reasons for trade barriers based on product characteristics.

As direct trade barriers become less available under the Uruguay Round agreement, there will be a natural tendency for governments to attempt to use other measures to substitute for quotas and tariffs. Under the new GATT rules, it will become more difficult to use sanitary and phytosanitary restrictions as substitutes when direct barriers are unavailable. This part of the agreement will not end disputes on these issues; it will, however, allow those disputes to be conducted within a framework of rules. No one expects the sanitary and phytosanitary agreement to lead to significant changes in trade policies or domestic programs. Reviews of current restrictions are being undertaken, but wholesale revisions should not be expected.

The sanitary and phytosanitary agreement may be the hardest part of the Uruguay Round for economists to analyze. The agreement sets out rules that prohibit arbitrary restrictions of imports based on unsubstantiated claims of human, plant, or animal health concerns. Reports of such restrictions have been widespread. No studies, however, show how much trade has been restricted by barriers with no scientific basis or even which barriers around the world are likely to be eliminated or reduced by the new rules.

The objectives of the United States for the sanitary and phytosanitary negotiations were to make it harder for trading partners to use unsubstantiated claims to block imports, while not undermining science-based rules protecting food safety and plant and animal health. The guidelines were established along the lines favored by the U.S. government and some U.S. export industries, particularly those exporting livestock and horticultural products. These industries expect to see more streamlined settlement of sanitary and phytosanitary issues under the new rules. Those in the fruit and vegetable trade, for example, expect this part of the Uruguay Round agreement to yield substantial benefits. They expect countries to hesitate to restrict trade arbitrarily if the World Trade Organization has a well-established mechanism for pursuing complaints against such measures. The major benefits from this part of the agreement may be that trade restrictions that would have been otherwise imposed are avoided. These effects will be hard to identify and especially hard to quantify.

Import Access. There are four parts to the access provisions:

1. Nontariff trade barriers will be converted to GATT-bound tariffs. The differences between internal and external prices during 1986–1988 are used as the basis for GATT-bound tariffs that provide equivalent protection to the nontariff barriers they replace. This tariffication was used to open the Japanese beef market a few years ago and was also used in NAFTA. Tariffication means that barriers such as the section 22 import quotas and the Meat Import Law in the United States and variable levies in the European Community are being converted to bound tariffs. In most cases nontariff barriers are replaced by two bound tariff rates. The first, low (or zero) tariff rate applies to the quantity of import access that was available during the base period. A second, higher tariff applies to any quantity of potential imports, in addition to the base-period quantity of imports. This two-tiered tariff, known as a tariff-rate quota, would initially limit imports to the base-period amount because the second-tier tariff is prohibitively high. The heights of the new tariffs are supposed to match the protection afforded by the nontariff barrier. This provision, while clear in principle, is vague enough that it provides ample room for dispute in its implementation.

Perhaps the most clear case of excess tariffs was in the tariffication of the Canadian dairy and poultry quotas. Tariffs in excess of 200 percent in some cases were created to replace quotas for products for which internal prices were at most 50 percent above border prices. With these excess tariff rates applied, no new trade opportunities arise from tariffication itself. The benefits from tariffication must therefore arise from the transparency of bound tariffs and the gradual reduction of tariff rates that will come during the continuation of Uruguay Round reductions after the initial liberalization period.

In the sole exceptions to universal tariffication, Japan and Korea were able to negotiate a delay in their implementation of tariffication for rice. In exchange for creating additional minimum import access during the implementation period, Japan will reconsider tariffication after six years. Korea provided additional access for other commodities and will reconsider tariffication for rice after ten years. Trading partners expect each country to accept tariffication for rice at that time.

Tariffication likely increased protection for a number of commodities in the short term. One reason for the next access provisions was to obtain some immediate benefit on access.

2. Agricultural tariffs will be reduced by an average of 36 percent over six years for developed countries and over ten years for developing countries. Each tariff line, including the newly created ones, will be reduced by at least 15 percent. The tariff agreement is for averages across tariff lines, and these averages are not weighted by trade flows. The tariff schedules in most nations include many tariff lines that are not used. Therefore it is likely that the reduction of the tariffs on politically sensitive commodities will be limited to the 15 percent minimum.

3. To ensure improved trade flows immediately in the most egregious cases, minimum import access for each commodity is required. The base requirement is that access be allowed at low or zero tariffs for at least 3 percent of base-period domestic consumption. The 3 percent figure is required to grow to 5 percent over the six-year imple-

mentation period. The initial draft of the Uruguay Round agreement specified that minimum access be ensured at the detailed four-digit level if possible and allocated back to tariff lines. This commodity-by-commodity access agreement, however, was not enforced for selected commodities in certain countries. The European Union, for example, did not follow these rules for pork and instead applied access rules to an aggregate of meat products. Further, for many commodities, consumption data are not available at this level of disaggregation so some adjustments on the original plans would be required anyway.

4. To ensure that the agreement does not make trade access worse, a provision was included to require that current access opportunities be maintained as a part of the tariffication process. (Current is defined as the average access during 1986–1988.) Since the amount of access that is now available is difficult to establish for many commodities, this provision also has room for various interpretations in its application. As discussed in some detail in chapter 4, the preexisting U.S. meat import law, for example, established a conditional quota but also a trigger mechanism that provided for "voluntary" restraints at a quantity of imports above the quota. New Zealand and Australia, major beef exporters, both complained that their effective access to the U.S. market has been reduced under the U.S. implementation of the Uruguay Round agreement because quota quantities rather than trigger quantities were used to establish the current access quantity in the U.S. implementation schedule.

Export Subsidies. Subsidized exports must be reduced by 21 percent in volume and 36 percent in budget outlays over six years from the 1986–1990 base period on a commodity-by-commodity basis. For commodities that experienced increases in the use of export subsidies after the base period, however, countries may phase in the export subsidy reductions in equal increments from 1991–1992 levels. Under these provisions products that did not receive export subsidies in the 1986–1990 period are ineligible for export subsidies in the future.

The quantity discipline on export subsidies was among the most contentious issues in the Uruguay Round negotiations. It also has important effects on projected world commodity prices and trade flows of major agricultural commodities, especially now that Common Agricultural Policy (CAP) reform has lowered the differential between internal European Union prices and world prices. It has been well understood that the quantity discipline had the potential to limit exports; thus EU negotiators demanded lower percentage cuts from those proposed by the United States and even from those included in the Dunkel Draft Final Act of 1991.

Throughout the negotiations the United States pushed for larger cuts in export subsidies than the EU was willing to tolerate. The final compromise, with a rate of quantity cut slightly smaller than in the Dunkel Draft Final Act (21 versus 24 percent, as per the Blair House accord) and an adjustment on the starting point for the cuts (using 1991 as a base rather than the 1986–1990 average, as in the final U.S.-EU bilateral agreement), must be considered minimal. Nonetheless, the quantity commitment will reduce subsidized exports significantly over the transition period and cause international prices to be somewhat higher than would otherwise be the case for most grains and livestock products. Further, the value commitment for a 36 percent reduction over six years, even if not binding initially, sets the stage for final elimination of export subsidies in three tranches, even if the reductions proceed at a slightly slower pace than 3 percent per year.

Internal Support Policies. Under the Uruguay Round the total of those domestic farm subsidies agreed as trade distorting (in the purely mercantilist sense that they tend to increase exports or reduce imports) must be reduced over six years by 20 percent from the 1986–1988 base period. Total support is measured by a single aggregate measure of support (AMS), which is the sum of commodity-specific AMSs and a sectorwide AMS. The policies not included in the AMS are included in the so-called green box of programs not subject to limitations. Conservation programs, research and extension, fully decoupled payments meeting strict criteria, and certain crop insurance and disaster aid programs are among those likely to qualify for the green box. These policies are also exempt from countervailing duty actions and such GATT challenges as nullification and impairment actions, as well as serious prejudice actions.

The agreement also exempts from the reduction in total support for the six-year implementation period certain direct payments that are made on a fixed quantity and on less than base-period production. These payments are not included in the AMS as long as payments are based on fixed areas and yields (or for livestock a fixed number of head) or payments are made on not more than 85 percent of the base production. These payments are not in the green box, but they are exempt from GATT challenges (other than countervailing duties), provided support for a specific commodity does not increase during the implementation period from 1992 levels.

The AMS calculates support based on fixed reference prices to measure changes in the influence of policy separately from the influence of movements in commodity markets due to such nonpolicy factors as weather. A *de minimis* level of 5 percent for developed countries and 10 percent for developing countries would be used for exemptions from reduction commitments.

Policies that qualify for green box exemption include service programs such as the following:

- Productivity-improving services. These include research, extension, training, pest control, inspection, marketing information and promotion, and infrastructure for transport, electricity, and water.

- Public stocks for food security.
- Domestic food aid.

Direct income aid to producers must meet several criteria and generally is expected to fall into one of the next eight categories:

1. decoupled income support so long as it is based on criteria defined for a fixed base period, is not related to volume of production or input use after the base period, and is not related to prices after the base period

2. income insurance or safety nets so long as the agricultural income loss exceeds 30 percent of gross income, or equivalent in net income, over a three-year average or the middle three of the last five years, payments cannot compensate for more than 70 percent of the lost income, and payments cannot be specific to type or amount of production, prices, or input use

3. disaster payments so long as an official disaster is declared, losses exceed 30 percent, payments do not exceed the amount of loss, and payments are not tied to future production

4. producer retirement programs that require total and permanent exits from agriculture

5. long-term resource retirement schemes under which land must be retired for at least three years, livestock must be permanently removed, and payments must not be conditional on using other land or on prices

6. investment assistance for which assistance levels are not related to prices or future production

7. environmental payments to compensate for meeting environmental or conservation regulations

8. assistance for disadvantaged regions so long as benefits are not related to prices or production but are linked to the extra costs of production in the disadvantaged area

Even a casual review of these criteria confirms that

these green box criteria have little relation to how much a policy or program would tend to increase exports or reduce imports. The list of green box policies was the result of several factors. First, the expected effects of most actual internal support programs on trade are relatively small compared with direct trade barriers or subsidies. Second, it is close to impossible to devise schemes to restrict indirect subsidies in all the variety that can be devised by clever bureaucrats. Third, internal political support for programs such as crop insurance, regional subsidies, and environmental subsidies is usually much stronger than the international support for restricting them. Therefore the programs and policies listed above were accepted in the green box even though their supply effects are likely to be at least as large as some direct income and price subsidies that were not included on the green box list. And, fourth, the operational significance of the green box list turned out to be minor in the final agreement except, perhaps, in the context of the peace clause.

The Peace Clause. The so-called peace clause places restraints on increasing commodity-specific subsidy rates. In particular, if (1) the direct payments that are exempt from reduction commitments conform with the agreement and (2) the amount of government support is not raised above that provided during the 1992 marketing year for the specific commodity, then these payments are exempt from GATT actions related to subsidies (article 16) or nullification and impairment. These direct payments that are exempt from reduction and other internal supports subject to reduction are not exempt from countervailing duty actions. The "nondistorting" permitted (green) policies are exempt from countervailing duty actions and other GATT challenges (for example, nullification and impairment actions, serious prejudice actions).

The specific language in the Uruguay Round on "peace" was among the most contentious elements. A trade war over peace was more than a remote possibility.

A key issue in interpreting the peace clause is to consider whether it can be used to protect trade practices that would have been subject to GATT disciplines before the Uruguay Round. Does the peace clause allow trade to be more distorted under the Uruguay Round rules than before? The distinction between the green box internal support policies and the category of nonreduced subsidies may become important in this regard. The peace clause may allow countries to undertake or expand policies that create trade barriers, free from the fear of legal actions. Under the Uruguay Round agreement, a whole list of agricultural policies now have formal multilateral acceptance. Most of these policies have some degree of trade-distorting effect and some of the most trade-distorting ones are on the list of green box policies. To exempt most of these policies from GATT challenge could make trade more distorted rather than less.

Further, it is not clear how successful the peace clause will be in keeping the peace when it is put under pressure. U.S. wheat farmers, for example, seem convinced that Canadian wheat is subsidized by a variety of domestic support programs that fall into the general category of revenue insurance. If the U.S. wheat industry is told that it cannot even contemplate taking an action against these Canadian policies because they have been declared green and are therefore exempt from challenge, the peace clause will be severely strained. A review of the recent International Trade Commission hearings transcripts provides a sample of views to help appreciate the attitudes of the U.S. and Canadian wheat producers (U.S. ITC 1994a). The expanding U.S. crop insurance program may raise similar concerns in other countries.

The Expected Effects of the Uruguay Round on U.S. Farm Exports. The United States has been a major trader in agricultural goods and has run a substantial trade surplus in agriculture for several decades (table 3–1). The

TABLE 3–3
PROJECTED INCREASE IN U.S. AGRICULTURAL EXPORTS UNDER
THE URUGUAY ROUND, FISCAL YEARS 2000 AND 2005
(millions of dollars)

Commodity	Change from Baseline[a]	
	FY 2000	FY 2005
Grains and feeds	490 – 1,940	1,950 – 3,910
Cotton	50 – 290	60 – 590
Animal products	740 – 1,660	1,690 – 2,510
Horticultural products	180 – 280	200 – 370
Oilseeds and products	170 – 530	810 – 1,330
Total	1,630 – 4,700	4,710 – 8,710

a. Fiscal year projections.
SOURCE: United States Department of Agriculture, Economic Research Service, Office of Economics, March 1994.

farm trade surplus is particularly large when one focuses on nontropical products for which the United States has a nonnegligible domestic industry (table 3–2). Therefore it is not surprising that the Uruguay Round agreement is expected to have a more significant impact on U.S. agricultural exports than on imports.

The effect of the Uruguay Round agreement on U.S. agricultural imports is expected to be slight. These import effects were mentioned above in the discussion of the import commitments. The only significant impacts are related to minimum access for dairy products and peanuts. These changes are discussed further in the next chapter.

It is convenient to use a table on export gains developed by the USDA (1994b) as a basis for discussion of the broad effects anticipated for U.S. agricultural trade. The USDA table is reprinted here as table 3–3. It shows export changes from the USDA baseline projections. This baseline includes the effects of EU policy changes included in the CAP reform that was implemented just before the Uruguay Round agreement was finalized in 1993. Therefore, although many observers attribute specific measures included in CAP reform to the pressures of the Uruguay Round negotiations, the reductions in EU exports attributable to CAP reform are not credited to the Uruguay Round agreement in the USDA analysis.

The values of exports listed in the table range 3 to 8 percent above the baseline levels by the year 2000. The expected expansion doubles from the year 2000 to 2005. These export gains are based on a combination of specific reductions in export subsidies by competitors, specific commitments on market access by customers, and the expected growth in world income from generally freer trade. The real growth in the gross domestic product is cumulative, and the USDA analysis is based on GDP in various countries being higher than they would otherwise be by one to three percentage points by the year 2000 and by two to eight percentage points by 2005 (USDA March 1994b, table 18). Since the specific agricultural commitments are all phased in by the year 2000, additional export gains from the years 2000 to 2005 attributable to the Uruguay Round are associated with faster economic growth.

For major grains the most significant factor underlying export growth by the United States is a decrease in subsidized exports by the EU. For rice the major factor is new access to markets in East Asia under the minimum access commitments. Livestock gains are from a combination of reduced EU subsidized exports, new access in Asia, and income growth worldwide.

The puzzle in the USDA table is the small expected gains in horticultural trade, which now makes up about $8 million of U.S. farm exports. The gain for horticultural products is expected to be only 2 to 4 percent even by 2005, when significant income elasticities of demand of these products in many of the importing countries should play a role.

Summary and Conclusions

This chapter has provided information on recent agricultural trade patterns and the international agreements that will shape those patterns in the coming years. The Uruguay Round agreement in particular has a global reach and will alter trade policy for most trading nations. In addition, the Uruguay Round agreement will mandate a number of specific changes required to bring U.S. agricultural trade programs and policy into compliance.

The current pattern of agricultural trade and the recent international agreements provide the basis for discussing specific agricultural trade policy and programs of the United States. This setting is used in the next two chapters. Chapter 4 describes and evaluates U.S. agricultural import policy, and chapter 5 is devoted to U.S. agricultural export policy. In both cases the current policy, recent changes, and potential reforms are placed in the context of NAFTA and, especially, the Uruguay Round agreement.

4
U.S. Agricultural Import Policy in the Wake of the Uruguay Round

This chapter begins with a review of recent agricultural import barriers in the United States and how these barriers were affected by the Uruguay Round agreement and NAFTA. Implementing legislation was required for each agreement to provide the specific changes to make U.S. law consistent with the commitments undertaken. This section also discusses some estimates of the costs and benefits of trade barriers in agriculture and provides a sense of the magnitude of the remaining barriers. The discussion of trade reform is complicated by certain policy changes that were adopted between the time of the Uruguay Round agreement and the time of the passage of the implementing legislation. Besides discussing import policy implied by the Uruguay Round agreement, this chapter highlights significant import policy changes made during 1994 that are counter to the spirit of the agreement.

At the same time that the implementation of the North American Free Trade Agreement and the Uruguay Round GATT agreement represented movements toward fewer trade barriers and subsidies, the United States has been taking steps in the opposite direction in selected industries. Some new barriers and subsidies were included in the Uruguay Round agreement itself, as in the case of the new tariff-rate quota for peanut butter and the new higher sugar tariff. And the levels at which nontariff barriers were tariffed was much above what an objective analysis of the data would have suggested. Some of the new measures, however, were undertaken outside the multilateral agreement and represent a further signal that protectionist pressure remains strong. Two of these, new trade barriers for tobacco and wheat, are discussed in some detail in the second and third sections of this chapter because they represent important protectionist deviations from the recent path towards more liberalization that has been undertaken by U.S. agricultural trade policy.

Current Import Policy and the Effects of Recent Trade Agreements

This section serves two purposes: it describes the current state of agricultural import policy in the United States, and it summarizes the influence of recent trade agreements on specific programs and policy parameters. Each category of import policy is discussed in turn.

Nontariff Barriers. When potential imports have been a major concern for a U.S. agricultural industry, nontariff barriers have often been used to provide protection from imports. This has been particularly true for commodities with a history of price and income support programs. Section 22 of the Agricultural Adjustment Act of 1933 (as amended) made specific provisions for import quotas for these commodities. These nontariff barriers are discussed in this subsection, and agricultural tariffs are discussed in the following subsection.

As noted in the basic descriptions of NAFTA and the Uruguay Round agreement provided in chapter 3, these agreements require that nontariff barriers be converted to tariffs. This procedure has already occurred (or is scheduled to occur) for imports from Mexico in the case of NAFTA. And while contentious during the negotiations and during the debate over implementing legislation, this NAFTA tariffication is expected to have relatively little impact on trade flows (Orden 1994). Mexico is not a major low-cost producer of the commodities for which the United States has had nontariff barriers.

The multilateral conversion of nontariff barriers to tariffs required by the Uruguay Round agreement will have a much more pervasive impact on trade policy in the United States than has the tariffication required by NAFTA. The commodities affected—sugar and sugar-containing products, beef, cotton, dairy products, and peanuts—are all politically important. If they were not, they would not have been able to maintain nontariff barriers for the past half century or more. In addition, beef and dairy are the two most important agricultural industries in the nation as measured by gross sales revenue. Tariffication under the Uruguay Round agreement means that the United States will apply tariff-rate quotas rather than strict quotas to potential imports from all nations that are signatories to the agreement.

The United States agreed to apply tariffication to sugar even though sugar imports have been restricted by a tariff-rate quota that was established in 1990 in response to a GATT panel finding. For sugar, the implementation actually allowed an increase in the tariff and a reduction in the expected access. Imports up to the quota amount pay a small duty of 0.625 cents per pound. A prohibitively high tariff of sixteen cents per pound (raw sugar) currently applies to any potential imports above the quota amount, which is adjusted yearly. The preexisting sugar tariff-rate quota policy was seen as unacceptable to trading partners during the Uruguay Round negotiations. The United States responded by undertaking a new tariffication of the sugar program arriving at a new higher tariff of seventeen cents per pound, which applies to all potential imports above 1.14 million metric tons. In addition section 22 quotas on selected sugar-containing products are being converted to tariffs.

U.S. sugar policy has long been held out as an example of a trade-distorting policy with substantial costs to consumers (Johnson 1974). The Uruguay Round agreement failed to cause any significant reduction in the excess costs of sugar to domestic consumers, at least in the short run. Nor did it reduce the excess resource cost of producing sugar in the United States when it could be imported at roughly half the cost. The price of sugar available on the world market varies but has remained in the range of about ten cents per pound compared with a little more than twenty cents per pound in the United States. If more import access was allowed, the domestic price would decline and the import price would rise slightly. The benefit of an expanded quantity of low-tariff imports of, say, 0.5 million tons of sugar would be a direct gain of about $100 million to consumers in lower outlays. The costs to growers and those who own sugar-producing land or other resources would be less than these gains to consumers because much of this sugar is produced at high cost on land that is environmentally fragile or better suited to other uses (Hafi et al. 1994).

Under the U.S. Meat Import Law, a quota level of beef imports varied each year, based on U.S. supply and demand factors. The law, however, also provided that no quota would be imposed unless projections of imports were more than 10 percent above the quota. This created an incentive for major exporters to negotiate "voluntary" restraint agreements to keep imports just under the quota trigger level but still almost 10 percent above the quota amount.

The tariffication of the Meat Import Law was the subject of substantial concern by exporting nations. Both the level of the initial tariff and the quantity in the first tier of the tariff-rate quota were of importance. As a result of a series of bilateral negotiations, mutually agreed quantities for the tariff-rate quota were established to set access no less than that provided under the existing nontariff barrier (NTB). Implementation of the Uruguay Round agreement replaces the previous system with a tariff-rate quota set at a quantity roughly equal to the earlier quota amount. The tariffs and quotas are shown in table 4–1.

For all tariffication items, the rate at which the NTBs were to be tariffied is controversial. Tariff equivalents of NTBs are certainly not straightforward in practice and that leaves considerable room for manipulation. Because both domestic prices and border prices vary by product characteristic, by date, and by other specifics of a transaction, it is easy to find data that make the difference between a border price and an internal price look large or small. An example from the negotiations of the U.S. beef tariff is instructive. At the Organization for Economic Cooperation and Development, exporting nations wanted to show that the U.S. Meat Import Law provided support to the U.S. beef industry. They encouraged the OECD to use a low border price and a high internal price for PSE calculations for U.S. beef. That was done, among other ways, by comparing Australian and New Zealand cow prices to U.S. prices. The result was a beef PSE in the range of 40 percent (OECD 1991). At the tariffication negotiations in the GATT, however, the roles were reversed. At this point the United States adopted a variant of the OECD approach to calculate tariff equivalents in the 30 to 40 percent range. The Australian and New Zealand negotiators were then in the position of repudiating the calculations they had successfully pursued, at least provisionally, at the OECD. They insisted on comparing beef of similar grade and quality with appropriate adjustments for transport and other associated costs. The final result is a tariff equivalent of 31 percent even though objective measurements

TABLE 4-1
Selected Tariff-Rate Quota Schedules under the Uruguay Round Agreement, 1995 and 2000

Product[a]	1995		2000	
	Quota (metric tons)	Overquota tariff	Quota (metric tons)	Overquota tariff
Beef and veal	656,621	31.1%	656,621	26.4%
Cotton	51,927	$0.37/kg	86,545	$0.31/kg
Peanuts	33,770		56,283	
In-shell		192.7%		163.8%
Shelled		155.0%		131.8%
Peanut butter	19,150	155.0%	20,000	131.8%
Dairy products[b]				
Cheese	110,999	$1.443/kg	141,991	$1.227/kg
Butter		$1.813/kg		$1.541/kg
Powder		$1.018/kg		$0.865/kg

a. New tariff-rate quotas are also provided for sugar and sugar-containing products.
b. For specific dairy product quotas by tariff line, see table 4-2.
SOURCE: United States Department of Agriculture, Foreign Agriculture Service, "GATT/Uruguay Round Fact Sheets," February 1994.

would suggest a tariff of no more than 10 percent.

More protection, not less, resulted from the Uruguay Round agreement for beef imports. The quantity allowed as imports at the low tariff rate is smaller than for imports in most years under the old law. Current access has been maintained only in a purely legalistic sense. Further, the tariff applied for the second tier is clearly excessive. The cost of beef import restrictions to U.S. consumers remains in hundreds of millions of dollars per year.

In the case of peanuts and some dairy products, minimum access at low initial tariffs implies increased imports compared with prior years. Dairy products are among the section 22 commodities with the most economic importance and political sensitivity. The final tariff schedules for dairy products were being adjusted up to the last weeks before the Marakesh meeting finalizing the agreement. The dairy minimum access quotas raise a number of complications. Several of the traded goods do not exist as domestically produced goods in the form imported. Some of these items were created as attempts to circumvent earlier NTBs. In addition, domestic consumption data are never available at the level of disaggregation in the tariff schedules. Therefore some aggregation in the numerators is required to create import shares to be used to set new import amounts to meet minimum access. Then the required adjustments in quotas must be distributed to individual tariff lines. Further, a substantial share of dairy consumption in the United States is in the form of fluid milk, which is generally not considered a tradeable good. Therefore the denominator for consumption of tradable dairy products in the minimum access calculations must be developed with care. The dairy product tariff-rate quotas are probably the most important and complex of the U.S. adjustments to the Uruguay Round agreement. Table 4–2 lists the new dairy trade barriers.

More dairy products will be imported as a consequence of the Uruguay Round agreement, but the quan-

TABLE 4–2

TARIFF-RATE QUOTA QUANTITIES FOR SPECIFIC DAIRY PRODUCTS
UNDER THE URUGUAY ROUND AGREEMENT, 1995 AND 2000
(in metric tons)

Product	Quota, 1995	Quota, 2000
Cream (liters)	5,801,600	6,768,500
Evaporated and condensed milk	3,000	7,000
Dried lowfat milk	1,500	5,500
Dried whole milk	550	3,500
Dried cream	100	100
Dried whey	300	300
Butter	4,000	7,000
Butter oil and substitutes	3,500	6,100
Dairy mixtures[a]	2,100	4,300
Chocolate crumb	16,000	26,700
Lowfat chocolate crumb	2,122.8	2,122.8
Milk replacer feed	7,400	7,400
Ice cream (liters)	3,576,112	5,960,186

NOTE: These tariff-rate quotas for dairy products account for an expansion in access from 13,700 to 22,785 tons of milk fat and an expansion from 16,100 to 26,825 tons of nonfat solids from the first year of the agreement to the year 2000.

a. 100 tons is set aside for infant formula containing oligosaccharides.

SOURCE: United States Department of Agriculture, Foreign Agriculture Service, "GATT/Uruguay Round Fact Sheets," February 1994.

tities are limited at best. In addition, the over-quota tariff levels are much higher than could be derived from objective data on potential imports and domestic sales. Remaining import barriers for manufactured dairy products help to keep domestic prices well above those of potential imports. Most of the U.S. domestic dairy industry could compete quite well on international markets, but the combinations of domestic price policy and import barriers make the domestic market and U.S. prices much more attractive than exports at international market prices. Some regions, especially New Zealand and a limited part of Australia, can produce tradeable dairy products at a lower cost than the United States. But the capacity of these regions is limited compared with the size of the world market. Therefore the appropriate long-term strategy for both consumers and producers of dairy products is to open the U.S. and other markets and to ban the use of dairy export subsidies. That action would cause higher international prices for dairy products, allow U.S. producers to compete in a nonsubsidized export market, and allow U.S. consumers access to additional low-cost dairy products.

Rucker, Thurman, and Borges (1994) have summarized the effect of the Uruguay Round on the U.S. peanut industry. U.S. peanuts are exported into the world market at competitive prices, but until Uruguay Round implementation, an import quota (set at near zero) allowed the domestic marketing quota to determine a domestic price that was well above the export price. Domestic consumption of peanuts under the domestic price support is a little more than half the crop of about 2 million tons, exports are about a quarter of the crop, and other uses make up the rest. Peanut prices for domestic edible use in the United States are about twice as high as the price of peanuts of similar quality on international markets. U.S. consumers pay about $300 per ton more than they likely would without the peanut program. The current program therefore costs domestic consumers on the order of $600 million in higher expenditures and additionally in terms of lost consumption opportunities. The U.S. peanut production industry would be a significant loser from an expansion of import access (USDA 1994b).

In its final and complete form, the Uruguay Round agreement did provide for some additional access for peanuts, but at the same time it added new barriers for processed peanut products (especially peanut butter from Canada). Therefore, under the new Uruguay Round policy, import access will probably increase significantly for peanuts and processed products taken together. An indication that access did not increase is that the U.S. peanut industry, which had vigorously opposed the Uruguay Round agreement until the final weeks of the negotiations, supported the agreement in its final form. Thus the tax on peanut consumers remains through the tariff-rate quota import barrier and the domestic price regulations and marketing quota that the import barriers make feasible.

Cotton is another major commodity with section 22 quotas. In the case of cotton, however, no additional imports are expected from the conversion to a tariff-rate quota because the current quota was not binding and the United States is a major cotton exporter of a wide variety of cotton qualities. The change in cotton import policy is of mainly symbolic interest and does little to affect the economics of the cotton industry.

Tariffs. Tariff protection is important for a number of items in U.S. agriculture. These include fruits and vegetables imported from Mexico on a seasonal basis, frozen concentrated orange juice, vegetable oils that compete with U.S. soybean oil, and a handful of other items.

Tariff reductions in the Uruguay Round agreement and NAFTA were controversial for several commodities in the United States that are protected solely by bound tariffs. Of particular political sensitivity were concentrated orange juice, fresh limes, and a few additional horticultural items. These items will all make use of the 15 percent minimum tariff cut allowed in the Uruguay Round agreement and may also find the safeguard provisions of interest. A number of these items also face added import competition from Mexico under NAFTA. Since the NAFTA tariff cuts are faster and go much further than those required in this tranche by the Uruguay Round agreement, it is not clear how much the Uruguay Round itself added to the import pressure. NAFTA tariff reductions will allow significantly more access for those items for which Mexico is an important source of supply. These products include winter tomatoes and a few other fruits and vegetables. In addition the cross-border movements of cattle will make that industry more efficient.

For many agricultural products NAFTA is of relatively little significance. The bottom line is that tariff protection remains of significance for several U.S. agricultural industries. These barriers allow higher prices for producers and cost consumers in terms of higher food prices. The net effect on the U.S. economy is a small but nontrivial net loss.

Sanitary and Phytosanitary Regulations. During the Uruguay Round negotiations, the United States vigorously pushed for a requirement that trade restrictions that claimed to be based on animal, plant, or human health concerns must be based on solid scientific evidence. Such a requirement was adopted. The expectation now is that no U.S. rules will be successfully challenged on this basis and that even when U.S. standards are more strict than international norms, they could be shown to have sufficient scientific basis. Relatively arbitrary barriers on imports have sometimes occurred, but the U.S. government has claimed in international negotiations that these instances are rare in the United States and much more common in other countries.

During the debate over implementation of the Uruguay Round agreement opponents raised the sanitary and phytosanitary chapter of the agreement, along with the new dispute settlement rules, as examples for which U.S. sovereignty would be particularly vulnerable. It is difficult to find a current or prospective sanitary or phytosanitary barrier in agriculture, however, that will be subject to change under the new rules. Import restrictions based on the use of pesticides or other chemicals that are considered safe in other parts of the world and have not been tested in the United States and thus are not on an approved list in the U.S. could be challenged. In these cases the fact that the United States pays relatively little attention to evidence derived from studies conducted in other countries may be subject to challenge.

A second category of potential challenges, or at least limits on domestic prerogative, concerns legislation that attempts to restrict imports based on environmental damage in another country or region. The examples raised, such as the U.S. ban on sale of tuna caught with the wrong type of nets, have never been claimed to be based on the issue of plant or animal health in the United States. The United States opposed the European Union's efforts to legitimize restrictions on how a product is produced under the sanitary and phytosanitary rules. It would not be legitimate, for example, under the current Uruguay Round agreement for the European Union to base its ban on dairy products produced by cows treated with bovine growth hormone on the welfare of the cows or on the effects on rural communities. The World Trade Organization would have no say in regulations on European production methods, but under this interpretation such domestic regulations would not be used to restrict imports.

Evaluation of the Import Provisions in the Uruguay Round Agreement. The principle that import barriers have a negative impact on the economy has been generally accepted and forms the economic basis for the gradual reduction of import barriers in NAFTA and the Uruguay Round GATT agreement. There are economic arguments that may provide a rationale for trade barriers in specific cases, but these arguments are not generally applicable in agriculture. In practice, continuation of import barriers for agricultural commodities is not generally supported by claims that specific import restrictions are good for the economy as a whole. Rather, the argument is that specific industries would be adversely effected by more competition from imports.

Most U.S. agricultural industries are in a strong position to compete internationally. For these industries import barriers provide protection for domestic farm program subsidies or facilitate policies to extract monopoly rents from domestic markets. Usually even supporters do not attempt to make general arguments for the benefit of import barriers to the economy as a whole.

Substantial import restrictions will remain after the implementation of the Uruguay Round agreement. These will cost consumers and the economy much more than the benefit to the specific agricultural industries that they protect. Whereas it is useful to pursue as much as possible a multilateral negotiation strategy, this need not limit unilateral reforms that strengthen the U.S. economy.

The New Tobacco Trade Barrier

Tobacco was initially considered a clear winner from the Uruguay Round. The United States has long been a major net exporter of tobacco and tobacco products even though imports comprise about one-third of a U.S. cigarette by weight. Domestic tobacco growers have been frustrated over the years by the quantity of low-priced foreign tobacco imported. But this frustration was moderated by the understanding that exports were more important than imports. Then, as the U.S. leaf tobacco export market declined over the past few years after doing well in the late 1980s, the pressure to restrict imports became intense.

Over recent decades the international market position of the U.S. leaf tobacco industry steadily eroded both in the export market and in the domestic market in competition with imports. Even with a declining export market share and increasing imports, however, the U.S. tobacco industry has found it profitable to maintain domestic production quotas and an essentially open border. The U.S. advantage in tobacco quality meant that the demand elasticities facing U.S. leaf continued to be relatively inelastic in both the domestic and the international markets (Sumner and Alston 1986, 1987; Alston and Sumner 1988).

A New Nontariff Barrier. Understanding the clear net benefits for the U.S. tobacco industry of the likely Uruguay Round GATT agreement was straightforward until the fall of 1993 (Sumner 1991; USDA 1992). The U.S. tobacco tariffs was generally low, and the United States did not use any nontariff barriers such as the section 22 quotas for peanuts or dairy products. Further, potential export growth has been substantial, and import markets for both manufactured products and leaf would expand with the agreement because of income growth and reduced barriers.

The implications of the Uruguay Round for tobacco became more complicated in the months leading up to the final Uruguay Round GATT agreement, when U.S. trade policy for tobacco changed. In the fall of 1993, a few months before the December 15, 1993, completion of negotiations for the Uruguay Round, the United States approved a new nontariff import barrier for tobacco. For 1994, cigarettes manufactured in the United States may not contain more than 25 percent imported tobacco. Thus the United States instituted a new agricultural nontariff barrier just two weeks after having successfully completed a seven-year campaign to ban nontariff barriers from international trade in agriculture. Zaini, Beghin, and Brown (1994) describe the policy and consider incentives for cigarette manufacturers to comply (see also Sumner [forthcoming]). Beghin and Sumner (1993) analyzed a similar domestic content rule for Australian tobacco but did not empirically evaluate the impacts.

Not only was the domestic content law inconsistent

with the Uruguay Round agreement, it was found to be a violation of existing GATT rules. The United States did not use its section 22 waiver or any other specific authority to provide a GATT-legal excuse for the law. Tobacco exporters argued that the U.S. law violates articles 3 and 11 of the GATT. The United States made no real legal defense of its new law but merely issued a statement that no "damage" was done to those wishing to export to the United States (a claim that Brazil disputed).

Analysis of the Content Rule. By placing a restriction on the factor mixture, the regulation causes cigarettes to be more costly. Manufacturers respond by producing less in total and by shifting some cigarette manufacturing offshore. Given that a substantial portion of domestic cigarettes are now exported, this second option may be quite important.

Figure 4–1 illustrates the trade-off between domestic and imported tobaccos in cigarette manufacture. Curve A shows the trade-off between imported and domestic tobacco in producing cigarettes. This curve has a tangent with the relative price line at point ˙ indicating domestic use Q_d. The content regulation, however, specifies that input use must lie on or below the diagonal line marked 75 percent. Therefore point ˙ is no longer feasible. Point a on curve A complies with the regulation, but moving to this point ignores the fact that the regulation would cause domestic manufacturers to produce less than quantity A. The result of the domestic content rule, then, is a move to points such as b or c on curves B or C. More domestic use would follow if the cigarette output decline were moderate. But a shift in output down to curve C implies less domestic use even though the domestic share increases to 75 percent of total tobacco use.

A preliminary draft paper by Zaini (1994) uses an equilibrium displacement model and parameters from earlier work to evaluate the effects of the content restric-

FIGURE 4–1
DOMESTIC CONTENT REGULATION AND DOMESTIC TOBACCO USE

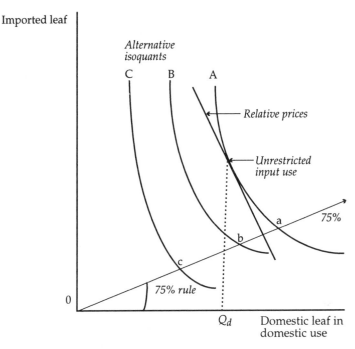

tion on U.S. tobacco demand, supply, price, and the income of producers. For his chosen parameters, Zaini's model indicates that the content law would raise the use of domestic tobacco and benefit U.S. tobacco producers. The substitution of domestic tobacco for imports would outweigh the reduction in total tobacco use.

The Zaini preliminary analysis uses an export demand elasticity for cigarettes of -3, an export demand elasticity for leaf tobacco of -2.33, a domestic demand elasticity for tobacco of -1, and an output elasticity (based on the setting of the production quota) of +1. These parameters imply a gain in domestic leaf price and quantity of about 4 percent. Domestic use of tobacco increases by about 11.5 percent, and exports fall by about 9 percent.

The Zaini analysis may overstate the benefit to U.S. leaf tobacco producers because its parameters tend to minimize the impact of the import barrier on the location of cigarette manufacturing and on the export market for U.S. leaf. In addition to domestic use of domestic tobacco, the new content regulation may adversely affect the market for U.S. leaf tobacco exports. Leaf importers may view the new U.S. trade barrier as a violation of the U.S. commitment to freer trade and respond with more trade barriers of their own.

The domestic content regulation or the new import barriers add constraints to U.S. cigarette manufacturers that may encourage a shift offshore, and as the domestic market shrinks, any export market retaliation by foreign countries becomes more important. Therefore, in the long run, the content policy or other import barriers may reduce total demand for U.S. leaf even if domestic demand shifts out a little and becomes more inelastic because of the constraint on import supply. Import barriers are dangerous for industries that rely on exports.

Even if the domestic leaf industry gains from the content restriction it is clear that the economies in tobacco-growing and cigarette-manufacturing regions lose. Even with an increase of 4 percent in domestic leaf use, the quantity of cigarettes manufactured falls by about 0.5 percent. That means less employment and revenue in the overall tobacco industry. In addition, tobacco leaf exports and cigarette exports both fall significantly.

The Conversion to a Tariff-Rate Quota. HR 5110, the implementing legislation for the Uruguay Round agreement, contains several provisions that revise import barriers for tobacco. Section 421 allows the authority to raise import barriers under GATT article 28: in the case of tobacco, negotiations to create new trade barriers and compensation for exporters can proceed. Section 422 modifies importer assessments along with domestic tobacco marketing assessments and allows the president to waive the domestic content law if he finds that it is in violation of any U.S. trade agreement (that is, GATT, NAFTA, or the new Uruguay Round agreement). This section also modifies the duty drawbacks for tobacco exports to make them more protectionist and to make them conform with the tariff-rate quotas likely to be created under the article 28 negotiations. These provisions in sections 422 are effective beginning with "the Presidential proclamation, authorized under section 421, establishing a tariff-rate quota pursuant to Article XXVIII."

The inconsistency implied by the U.S. instituting a nontariff barrier for a major export industry just when other such barriers in the United States and elsewhere are being dismantled (in part because of U.S. insistence) is particularly ironic given that the U.S. tobacco industry has operated a successful cartel and has a future that depends on exports. This new domestic content law caused trade friction, and the new barriers under article 28 will not undo that damage to the tobacco industry or to the effectiveness of the United States in negotiations for more open markets in other countries.

The New Wheat Trade Barrier

The United States has long been a major wheat exporter but has nonetheless occasionally applied restrictions on wheat imports. Despite, or perhaps because of, a free trade agreement that went into force in 1989, in recent years the political pressure for additional import restrictions on wheat imports from Canada has been intense. The administration succumbed to such pressure in the middle of 1994.

After the Uruguay Round negotiation was settled but before implementing legislation was passed, the United States and Canada temporarily resolved a continuing wheat trade dispute by agreeing to a voluntary import restraint agreement on wheat entering the United States. The United States promised to impose no temporary unilateral barriers (under section 22) and to suspend seeking a permanent new wheat tariff under article 28 of the GATT if Canada would agree "voluntarily" to restrict wheat exports to the United States for the year from August 1994 to July 31, 1995.

Canada agreed that any imports above the separate quota quantities for durum and other wheat would be subject to high and likely prohibitive tariff rates per ton. Thus, this "voluntary" restraint takes the form of a tariff-rate quota and is officially two tariff rates and not a nontariff barrier. Further, since it is a "voluntary" restraint, no GATT sanctions apply.

The Long-standing Bilateral Dispute. The United States undertook a section 22 proceeding to block wheat imports in early 1994. The section 22 case followed several unsuccessful efforts to block durum imports on the basis of Canadian subsidization of wheat production and implicit export subsidies (Alston et al. 1994; U.S.-Canada Binational Panel 1993; U.S. International Trade Commission 1994b). Under the Uruguay Round agreement, the United States is giving up its long-standing GATT waiver that allowed it to institute new tariffs and quotas without providing compensation to those adversely affected. The U.S. implementing legislation for the Uruguay Round agreement states that section 22 is amended so that it no longer applies to commodities produced by countries that are members of the WTO. The effective date of this provision is the date that the WTO agreement goes into force, except that the effective date for ending section 22 is delayed until September 12, 1995, for wheat. Thus the United States has maintained its domestic legal authority to apply unilateral barriers on Canadian wheat imports for several additional months.

This case is important in part because it highlights

the stress that open borders place on export subsidy programs. Conversely, the U.S. imports of wheat and those of barley and a few other commodities show how export programs make it difficult to comply with agreements to open the border to imports. For peanuts, sugar, and dairy products, domestic price support programs make it difficult for the United States to have low import barriers. Under the high loan rate policies of earlier decades, this was also true for grains. Since the 1990 FACT Act, however, the domestic wheat program has been mainly composed of (almost) decoupled direct payments, and any significant market price boost is provided by export subsidies (see chapter 5).

There is little puzzle why imports of wheat have increased in recent years. The real questions are why imports from Canada have not risen by even more and why wheat imports from Argentina and other suppliers have not occurred. Chapter 5 considers the U.S. wheat export subsidy program in some detail. The U.S. export subsidy provides $40 per ton or more as an added incentive to ship U.S. wheat offshore. This subsidy depresses the price in these international markets and raises the U.S. domestic market price. While transport costs may provide some natural import protection for the United States, trade barriers or some other limit must be in place to keep out foreign supplies when U.S. prices rise past a certain level relative to prices elsewhere. Imports of grain from Canada have been surprisingly moderate given the differential between the price in the U.S. market and other export markets used by Canada.

The U.S. International Trade Commission (USITC) began its 1994 investigation on wheat under section 22 of the Agricultural Adjustment Act of 1933 (as amended) in January after the president, to secure votes in favor of NAFTA, had promised several Congressmen that he would pursue the issue. The USITC was asked to investigate whether imports of wheat and wheat flour had interfered, or were practically certain to "materially interfere," with the U.S. price and income support programs for wheat, and to make recommendations concerning what actions the president might take. The dispute centered on how great the impact of imports were and whether this was enough to constitute material interference.

The Impact of Wheat Imports. The U.S. government's case for material interference was based primarily on the observation that deficiency payments are determined by the domestic market price of wheat and that imports increase supply available in the domestic market and consequently reduce the market price and increase the government outlays for the wheat program. The Department of Agriculture claimed that the price-depressing effect of wheat imports caused an additional $200 million in annual deficiency payments (Collins 1994).

The economic argument to the contrary was simply that, under the current conditions in the wheat market, such a price effect was likely to be slight. In research prepared for the Canadian Wheat Board, Sumner, Alston, and Gray (1994) developed an empirical model of the wheat market and simulated the effects of imports and import restrictions on the price of wheat and expected outlays on deficiency payments. The model indicated that eliminating wheat grain imports in 1993–1994 would have increased the price of wheat by about $0.01 per bushel and would have reduced deficiency payments by about $20 million dollars, or about 1 percent. Recently Haley (1994) has presented a USDA report that suggests that blocking imports would reduce the price of wheat in the United States. (Also see Alston, Gray, and Sumner [1994] for a comparison of estimates.)

The wheat trade dispute is the headline case in recent attempts by the United States to restrict imports while concurrently using trade agreements to attempt to open markets multilaterally. To understand how this case evolved and the importance of trade to the U.S. wheat market, it is worth summarizing the analysis in Sumner, Alston, and Gray. For a more thorough discussion of the USDA analysis, see Alston, Gray, and Sumner (forthcoming).

Total wheat imports into the United States were about 3.7 percent of market supplies for 1993–1994 and are expected to fall to about 2.5 percent for the 1994–1995 crop year. (This projection, made by the USDA before the recent binational wheat agreement, was unaffected by the newly created "voluntary" export restraint.) Imports serve three distinct markets in the United States: durum wheat is used for pasta, other milling wheat is used for baked goods, and low-quality wheat is used for livestock feed in competition with corn and other feed grains.

Within these categories, wheat from one origin often has distinct characteristics and is imperfectly substitutable with wheat from other origins. Characteristics of the grain itself or marketing specifics differ by origin. As a result, wheat produced in the United States or Canada, for example, can sell for somewhat different prices, and a slight rise in the price of one does not cause its market to evaporate. The Sumner, Alston, and Gray model uses Armington (1969) assumptions to specify the substitution relationships in the simulation model.

The United States uses durum, other milling wheat, and feed wheat from domestic production and from Canada. The United States also imports durum in the form of pasta (mainly from Europe). Import of pasta products from Europe is important and growing. This pasta is included (in wheat-equivalents) in official USDA data on durum trade. Trade restrictions have not been applied to these pasta imports, and pasta imports consequently expand as other imports are lowered. In international markets, wheats from Canada, the United States, and other origins all compete as closely related but not identical products. For feed use, the major competition comes from other grain and nongrain livestock feeds; wheats from different origins are almost perfect substitutes for one another.

The U.S. wheat market is closely connected to other markets in the world mainly because the United States is the world's largest wheat exporter. Canada is also a major wheat exporter to international markets, where U.S. and Canadian wheat compete directly. Lower U.S. imports mean more supplies from Canada to international markets and consequently more competition for U.S. exports. The U.S. domestic market price is higher than the effective export price from the United States because the EEP provides per unit subsidies to make up the difference between the domestic price that exporters must pay to acquire wheat in the United States and what the wheat can sell for in the export market.

Limits on wheat grain imports cause a series of reactions in the wheat market in the United States, including changes in production, domestic use, exports, and imports of pasta. Lower imports into the United States also cause wheat to be more abundant in international markets because shipments previously sent to the United States are diverted.

The implications of restricting wheat imports are determined largely by the important role of the United States in the world wheat market and by the fact that restricting imports from Canada diverts that wheat and causes a slightly weaker market for U.S. exports. In addition, imports of wheat used as feed have relatively little price effect because feed wheat makes up only a few percentage points of the total feed grain market and imports make up only a portion of the feed wheat component. Finally, imports of durum wheat in the form of pasta continue and even expand when durum grain imports are restricted.

Based on a simulation of restricting wheat grain imports to half the actual total for 1993–1994, the following quantitative implications were found:

- Pasta imports would have been about 30 percent higher.
- Production would have been up only slightly.
- U.S. exports would have been lower to make up the shortfall in the domestic market and to adjust to the more competitive international market. Durum exports would have been down by 15 percent. Other milling wheat exports would have been 1 percent lower.
- Market prices would have been only slightly higher for each type of wheat.
- The average market price received by producers (the average used for deficiency payments) would have been higher by a half cent per bushel: from $2.97 to $2.975.
- Outlays for deficiency payments would have been about $9.9 million (0.5 percent) lower.

Temporary Resolution of the Dispute. The USITC reviewed information from the USDA, Canadian respondents, U.S. wheat producers, U.S. millers, pasta makers and other industry interests, and its own staff. It forwarded its findings and recommendations to the president on July 15, 1994. In section 22 cases, ITC findings only provide information to the president: they have no binding impact on any decision. Three of the six commissioners (including the chairman and vice-chairman) reported as a group that they had determined no "material interference" with the U.S. wheat program by imports. These commissioners, however, did provide the president with recommended import restraints should he have determined (contrary to their findings) that there were grounds for restricting imports. A fourth commissioner determined that there was sufficient evidence to determine material interference but recommended only that a 10 percent additional duty should be applied after imports of durum reached 500,000 tons and of other wheat, 800,000 tons. Such a policy would have been unlikely to have had any significant impact on imports. The last two

commissioners also found material interference and recommended that relatively tight tariff-rate quotas should
be applied.

Before the president took any action relative to the
section 22 case, the wheat trade dispute between Canada
and the United States came to a negotiated resolution, at
least for the 1994–1995 year. At the end of July 1994, the
government of Canada agreed to limit wheat exports to
the United States, and the United States agreed to drop
its efforts to secure an article 28 action under the GATT to
restrict wheat imports. The terms of the "voluntary" export restraint follow:

• Canada may export up to 300,000 metric tons of
durum and 1.05 million metric tons of other wheat from
the Canadian Wheat Board regions of Western Canada
during 1994–1995 without added restrictions.

• Wheat from the rest of Canada, wheat flour, and
semolina are also subject to no new restraints.

• For shipments between 300,000 and 450,000 tons,
durum will be subject to a tariff of $23 per ton.

• For durum shipments above 450,000 tons and for
other wheat shipments above 1.05 million tons, the tariff
is $50 per ton.

• During the year under which these restraints are
in force, a commission of nongovernmental experts will
work to resolve the wheat trade issue.

Whereas these restraints may well influence the ex
post quantity of export shipments during the twelve-
month period covered by the agreement, it is instructive
that the official USDA projections for wheat imports during the 1994–1995 marketing year remained at 80 million
bushels (2.4 million tons) before and after the agreement.
The agreement was not viewed as a binding constraint
on expected U.S. imports by the USDA analysts, except
for durum. The total projected imports are well above the
level of imports of grain from Canada because shipments

from other national sources are significant for wheat imported in the form of products such as pasta. After all the effort and the significant symbolic inconsistency exhibited by U.S. trade policy, the quantitative result in this case is likely to be no significant effect on wheat imports, at least over the life of the one-year agreement.

Conclusions

For products for which some reform was accomplished in the Uruguay Round agreement, the key to reform is to continue the process on a multilateral or a unilateral basis. In some cases, as domestic price support and subsidy programs are reformed, import barriers can be relaxed as well. In other cases the removal of the import barriers can provide the impetus for domestic subsidy reform.

One issue for the 1995 farm bill is how to deal with import pressure without reverting to new protectionist measures. One obvious answer is to reduce the export subsidies that generate the price wedge between the U.S. domestic and export markets. Lower export subsidies by the EU, and by Canada in the form of reduced transport subsidies, are expected to provide higher export prices for wheat and other grains as the Uruguay Round takes effect. The 1995 farm bill could enhance those export price increases by reducing EEP quantities and bonus levels more rapidly than required by the Uruguay Round agreement. A multilateral agreement for accelerated implementation of the reductions negotiated in the Uruguay Round would mean even greater price increases.

5

An Evaluation of Export Programs and Trade Policy

Explicit export programs have long been a part of agricultural policy in the United States. In recent years the importance of export aid has increased as explicit price subsidies have replaced food aid as the most significant export program and as commercial exports have become a more important source of demand for more commodities. Export policy interacts closely with domestic subsidy policy for some commodities. In an effort to increase commodity prices, for example, programs to shift out the demand curve by subsidizing or otherwise promoting exports can substitute for programs that shift back the supply curve by requiring land to be idled. Just as was the case with import policies in chapter 4, this chapter attempts to evaluate export policies in the context of related domestic subsidies without a full evaluation of all policies jointly. The idea is to highlight the consequences of the export subsidies themselves while acknowledging where interactions with other policies are particularly important.

This chapter focuses on the consequences of export price subsidies, credit subsidies, marketing subsidies, and food aid. All these policies and programs act to increase exports by using government assistance, but they differ in the form of the aid or the international markets that they target. These policies and programs are also treated differently in international agreements. The chapter reviews the important issues in the context of recent domestic policy changes and in the wake of the Uruguay Round agreement to phase down selected export subsidies but not others. I begin with the explicit price subsidies that have become particularly important in the past decade.

Direct Export Price Subsidies

Export price subsidy reform is the most important trade policy issue facing U.S. agriculture. The United States conducted a decade-long campaign to eliminate export subsidies in agriculture and has long argued in general that export subsidization has no place in international trade. At the same time the United States has aggressively used export subsidies for several industries. There have been a number of conceptual arguments for why export subsidies may be justified as contributing to national welfare in addition to contributing to the income of specific farm interests. The administration has now committed itself to maintaining export subsidies to the full extent allowed by the Uruguay Round agreement no matter what the effect on the American economy. This issue is so important and so contentious that substantial space and detailed analysis are devoted to it in this section.

Export subsidies have been used by the United States intermittently for many years. They were first authorized under the original Agricultural Adjustment Act (AAA) of 1933. In the first instance, export subsidies were applied to wheat and wheat flour. Sixty years ago funds for export subsidies were provided under section 32 of the AAA amendments of 1935. Section 32 provided that 30 percent of tariff receipts be used to encourage the export or domestic consumption of agricultural commodities (Johnson 1950). Until 1974 these funds were often used to subsidize exports and may still be used for this purpose at the discretion of the secretary of agriculture. Recently section 32 funds have been used mainly for domestic purchases and food distribution programs and for selected export subsidies.

Export subsidies have also been authorized under various ad hoc schemes and agreements such as the International Wheat Agreement of 1949. In that case the domestic price support for wheat was above the maximum export price allowed under the agreement. The government provided the difference between the U.S. domestic price and the agreed international maximum export price (Benedict and Stine 1956; Ackerman and Smith 1990). As we shall see, wheat is currently a major commodity for subsidized exports as well.

Description of Current Programs. Since the collapse of U.S. agricultural exports in the early 1980s, export subsidy programs have become particularly important and contentious. In 1985 the United States introduced a new round of export subsidies under the Export Enhancement Program. The EEP began operation under the continuing charter authority of the Commodity Credit Corporation. It was subsequently authorized under the 1985 Farm Security Act. At first the EEP provided export subsidies in the form of commodities from CCC inventory, but as these inventories became depleted, the program continued by providing cash subsidies. (See Ackerman and Smith [1990] and Gardner [1994] for a history of the EEP program.)

The EEP covers a number of commodities, but in practice it has been used most for wheat and flour. The Dairy Export Incentive Program was also authorized under the 1985 act to provide bonuses, initially in the form of commodity certificates and now in the form of cash, to exporters of dairy products. Subsequent to the 1985 act, several commodity-specific export subsidy programs were introduced. The Sunflowerseed Oil Assistance Program was authorized in 1988, and the Cottonseed Oil Assistance Program began in 1989. Section 32 funds have been used for these programs in recent years.

The importance of export subsidies varies widely even among the commodities to which they have been applied (table 5–1). Only a tiny share of rice, beef, or pork exports, for example, is made under EEP. Conversely, almost all barley and more than half of all egg, vegetable oil, and wheat exports have recently been made under the applicable export subsidy programs.

Several additional characteristics of current export subsidy programs, including the following, should be taken into account in any discussion of reform:

• The subsidy is targeted on a subset of the total export market. In particular the subsidies have not been provided to Japan, Korea, Taiwan, the EU, or much of Latin America.

• The subsidies are no longer provided in-kind from government stocks. They are provided in cash to the U.S. export firms.

• The EEP process within the government requires first that individual national markets be judged eligible.

• After a market receives an EEP allocation, per unit price subsidies to eligible markets vary by transaction.

The program is designed so that export firms deal with export buyers directly to determine the export subsidy required to complete a sale. The proposed per unit subsidy is evaluated to determine if it is the minimum necessary for the given transaction in the eligible market.

These programs that apply direct export price subsidies are subject to the Uruguay Round agreement disciplines

TABLE 5-1
U.S. URUGUAY ROUND AGREEMENT COMMITMENTS REGARDING EXPORT SUBSIDIES, 1995 AND 2000

Commodity	Annual Quantity (metric tons)		Annual Outlay ($1,000)	
	1995	2000	1995	2000
Wheat	20,238,000	14,522,000	765,490	363,815
Coarse grains	1,906,000	1,561,000	67,735	46,118
Rice	272,000	39,000	15,706	2,369
Vegetable oil	587,538	141,299	52,960	14,083
Butter, butter oil	42,989	21,097	44,793	30,497
Skim milk	108,227	68,201	121,119	82,464
Cheese	3,829	3,030	5,340	3,636
Other milk	12,456	34	14,374	21
Beef	21,486	17,589	33,520	22,822
Pork	483	395	730	497
Poultry	34,196	27,994	21,377	14,555
Eggs	30,262	6,920	7,588	1,604

SOURCE: U.S. Department of Agriculture, Foreign Agriculture Service, "GATT/Uruguay Round Fact Sheets," February 1994.

on export subsidies, discussed in chapter 3. For each commodity, subsidized export quantities in the year 2000 must be 21 percent below the average during the 1986 to 1990 base period. In addition the value of export subsidies must be reduced by 36 percent compared with the base period values for each commodity. The schedule of reductions requires that export subsidies be cut in equal installments from either the 1986–1990 base or from the 1991 levels if export subsidies in that year were higher than they were in the base period. The commitments are noted in table 5–1 for each commodity.

The size of the implied reductions compared with current exports or the 1995 commitment depends on the quantity of subsidized exports and the value of export subsidy for that commodity in the base period. The wheat commitment on a tonnage basis, for example, requires a reduction of about 30 percent by the year 2000 from recent quantities subsidized and a reduction of more than 50 percent in the value of export subsidies for wheat from 1993 EEP outlays for wheat. Because the quantity of wheat subsidized averaged about 18 million metric tons in the base period and because average per unit bonuses were below those experienced more recently, the cuts in quantities and especially in total outlays are substantially larger than 21 and 36 percent when calculated on the basis of current program levels. This issue is seen much more dramatically for commodities such as rice and other milk products, for which there was relatively little use of export subsidy programs during the 1986 to 1990 period.

Conceptual Arguments for Targeted Export Subsidies. Export price subsidies have been the subject of a vigorous academic and political debate in recent years. (See, for example, Abbott et al. [1987]; Alston, Carter, and Smith [1993]; Anania et al. [1992]; Dutton [1990]; and USDA [1986].) Almost all analysis to date has focused on the EEP, especially the effects of the EEP for wheat. The export subsidies for other commodities are similar, and the same conceptual issues apply to them.

U.S. export subsidy programs (EEP, DEIP, COAP, and SOAP) can be examined relative to a number of criteria or objectives. These include their success at increasing (a) farm income for producers of the commodities targeted; (b) income in the U.S. commodity industry, including firms involved in farm supply and marketing; (c) income in agriculture as a whole, including nonsubsidized commodities that may compete with subsidized exports and livestock producers that may be affected by subsidized grain exports; and (d) net national income. Most research to date has taken a rather limited set of impacts to analyze and has focused on the short run, with impacts examined and measured mainly in the years in which the subsidies occur.

The most interesting issue to examine is the effect of export subsidies on national income. Several conceptual arguments related to export subsidies could support the idea that targeted export subsidy programs increase national income. The first relates to terms of trade gains in the nonsubsidized export market. If the market demand in the nonsubsidized export market is less elastic than the subsidized export market, then quantity falls only slightly as price rises, and substantial revenue is gained by raising the export price to this market. A significant revenue or net income gain in the nonsubsidized market requires that the subsidy create large additional quantities of exports and that this added quantity cause a large domestic supply price increase.

The second conceptual argument for export subsidies relates to their potential to lower the total budget cost of the combination of domestic and export subsidies for wheat. In some cases, other program costs may decline when export subsidies are expanded. By shifting out total demand, a targeted export subsidy raises the domestic price to producers. When this price is also used to calculate the domestic farm program payments, part of the potential gain to producers is instead transferred back to taxpayers as lower outlays for the domestic subsidy. Conceptually the domestic price increase can be large enough so that the savings in domestic program costs more than offset the expenditures on the export subsidies. Then, if the deadweight cost of taxation is large enough, the export subsidy can actually increase national welfare. This conceptual argument is discussed in some detail below for the current EEP program.

When the EEP program was initiated in 1985, the potential for lowering total government outlays was more likely because EEP export subsides were made in the form of wheat removed from government stocks. Per unit government storage costs were extremely high, and program rules precluded simply releasing the stocks on the market. By releasing wheat that would have otherwise continued to sit in storage facilities, the EEP reduced government storage costs. In the current situation the EEP has little, if any, impact on government stockholding; therefore direct farm payment savings must be compared directly with the additional export bonus payments.

A third conceptual argument for export subsidies relates to mitigating the economic resource cost of the domestic farm payment scheme rather than the budget costs. In particular, the amount of land required to be idled under the farm program may be reduced in response to an increase in demand caused by the export subsidy. In that case the national welfare losses associated with land idling are smaller, and this improvement may offset the economic cost of the export subsidy. For such an argument to be quantitatively important, the welfare losses from idling land must be significant, and the elasticity of demand in the export market must be relatively large.

Before we examine the direct economic and budget consequences of export subsidies in more detail, it is also useful to consider an argument in favor of export subsidies as strategic trade policy tools. It is often argued that the EEP, for example, may have contributed to the EU reform of the Common Agricultural Policy (CAP) and to the reduction of EU export subsidies through Uruguay Round commitments. It is true that policy changes implied by CAP reforms and the Uruguay Round agreement entail long-term future gains for the U.S. wheat industry through higher future prices in world markets and a larger quantity of U.S. commodity exports (USDA 1994b). In addition the benefits of the Uruguay Round agreement are much broader than the wheat industry or even agriculture. Therefore, if a significant share of the credit for an agreement could be attributed to the EEP program and the pressure it created toward multilateral reform, then the past EEP outlays may have more than paid for themselves.

The 1990 FACT Act explicitly required the use of the EEP and related programs to counter unfair trade practices. Further, the 1990 Omnibus Budget Reconciliation Act tied spending for export programs directly to progress in the Uruguay Round. The act required that spending on export programs increase if the round were not successfully concluded by June 1992. This threat did not succeed, and the required additional outlays were made.

Using export subsidies as a trade negotiation tool makes sense only if the degree of pressure placed on foreign governments from the export subsidy is intense enough to affect the path of policy reform significantly. The intensity of the pressure depends on how much the export subsidy reduces prices in international markets or reduces the exports of targeted competitors. The key target for the EEP was the EU export subsidy program. (See de Gorter and Milke [1987] for a discussion.) There is some evidence that the budget costs of EU export subsidies were higher because of U.S. export subsidies, particularly on a per unit basis. Because the EU provides subsidies on the total amount of its wheat exports, anything that lowers export prices causes them to make substantially higher outlays to maintain exports. But lower export prices also reduce the direct benefit of export subsidies for the United States wheat industry.

Policy pressure on the other subsidizing exporters can coexist with large export gains by the United States if the expansion of U.S. exports replaces foreign exports and the export price declines little. In that case these missed export sales by foreigners are reflected in increased stocks or reduced production in the foreign country. There is some evidence that this occurred in Europe in the early 1990s.

While the potential benefits associated with the negotiations may have been large in the Uruguay Round, their magnitude is obviously speculative. To the extent that export subsidies may have been useful in the past, they now have slight potential to encourage further international reforms. Further, export subsidies have other international policy consequences that should be considered. In particular, the export subsidies may adversely affect nonsubsidizing nations that are generally trade allies of the United States. From a long-term trade policy perspective, it may be detrimental to offend these countries for short-term market gains. Countries such as Argentina, which is important in wheat trade, or New Zealand, which is important in world dairy product trade, do not have the policy clout that comes with large domestic markets, but they do play significant roles in multilateral negotiations. These countries are in a strong position to emphasize the hypocrisy of U.S. agricultural trade policy, particularly if export subsidies are directed toward competing with them for markets that are otherwise not subsidized.

A second and more ironic strategic argument for export subsidies is based on monopoly power in wheat trading. This case for subsidies in wheat trade is not that they help U.S. farmers compete with Australian or European wheat farmers. Rather, the argument is that export subsidies allow the U.S. divisions of Cargill or Louis Dreyfus to make more profit in wheat trading at the expense of the Australian Wheat Board or the European divisions of Cargill or Louis Dreyfus. The goal would be to use government subsidies to drive the competitors out of business and thereby increase monopoly returns for U.S. exporters. Some have claimed that more profits for multinational trading companies were the inadvertent result of some U.S. farm policies (and some have even claimed that this was the nefarious hidden purpose of trade subsidies), but no one has claimed (in public) that such profits were the legitimate aim of farm trade policy.

The Policy Context and Parameters Affecting Export Subsidies. Any evaluation of a complex commodity policy such as the EEP hinges on what other policies and market conditions are expected to hold independently of the policy evaluated. In particular, in the case of the EEP, one must first decide how the income and price support programs are likely to respond to adjustments in the EEP. Alternative policy adjustments are worth reviewing because the analysis differs under alternative domestic policy responses and we do not know which policies will be pursued.

In addition to alternative policy responses, evaluation of the effects of export subsidies depends on a few key supply and demand parameters. One important parameter related to the success of export subsidies is how the quantity exported responds to the subsidy. It is well known and accepted that some subsidy will be paid on export sales that would have been made even without the subsidy. In these cases the subsidy was unnecessary and a pure gain to the foreign buyers. The additional export quantity created by the EEP, known as its additionality, is key to raising the domestic price for producers and lowering outlays for the domestic wheat deficiency payment program. Unfortunately, solid evidence with respect to EEP additionality remains elusive. Depending on competitive conditions, the EEP export bonus per ton of wheat has varied widely from year to year and market to market. The share of wheat sold under the EEP program has grown over time but has also varied from year to year. Based on these factors and on varying conditions in world markets, reasonable estimates of additionality have ranged from as high as 40 percent to close to zero. (See Anania et al. [1992]; Alston, Carter, and Smith [1993]; Gardner [1994]); and especially GAO [1994] for reviews of the empirical literature on this topic.) It has even been argued that cumbersome EEP procedures may have actually reduced U.S. wheat exports to some markets from what they would have been without the potential subsidy. On occasion, export firms may have missed out on potential sales while waiting for approval of bonuses when they might have made the sale had they known initially that no subsidy of the amount proposed was to be available.

Graphical Analysis of Export Subsidies. Figures 5–1 and 5–2 illustrate targeted export subsidies and decoupled deficiency payment programs operating simultaneously. Figure 5–1 illustrates the case in which the Acreage Reduction Program (ARP) is constant so the supply curve does not shift in response to the institution of the export subsidy program. Supply responds to a higher market price along the relatively inelastic market supply function. Figure 5–2 illustrates the case in which domestic policy responds to the export subsidy program by allowing more acreage to be planted under the domestic wheat program. This figure shows the results when acreage expands enough so that the domestic market price does not rise with more exports.

These figures allow the examination of some key features of the U.S. export subsidy policy operating in

FIGURE 5–1
TARGETED EXPORT SUBSIDY WITH DECOUPLED DOMESTIC DEFICIENCY PAYMENTS AND CONSTANT ARP

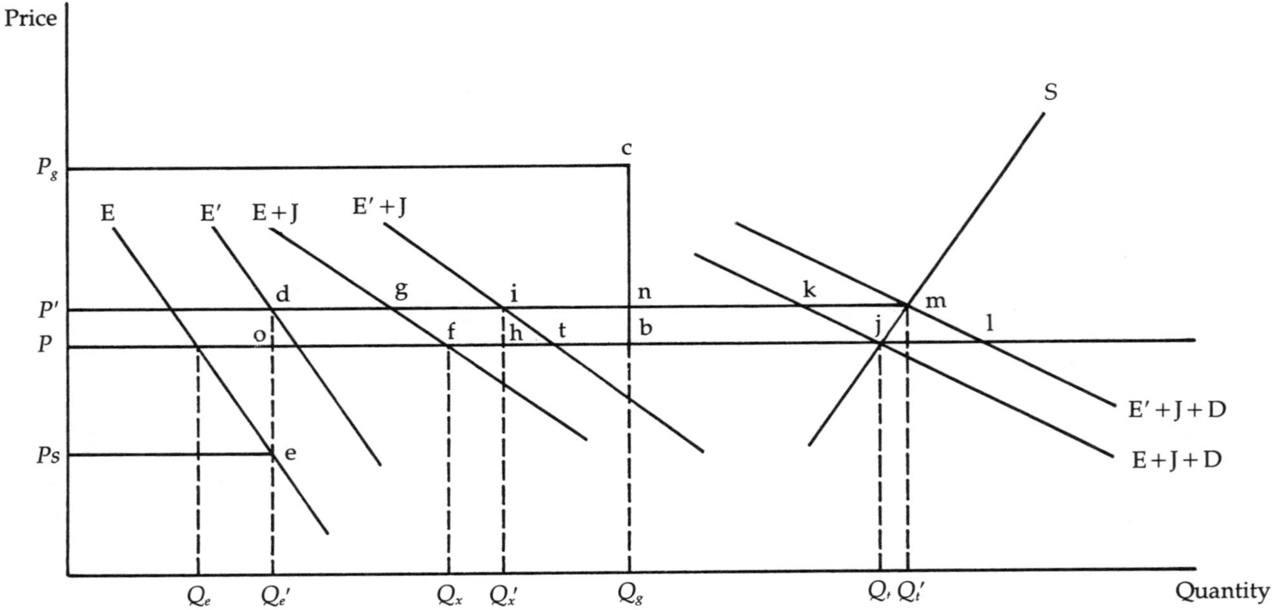

FIGURE 5-2

Targeted Export Subsidy with Decoupled Domestic Deficiency Payments and ARP Adjustments

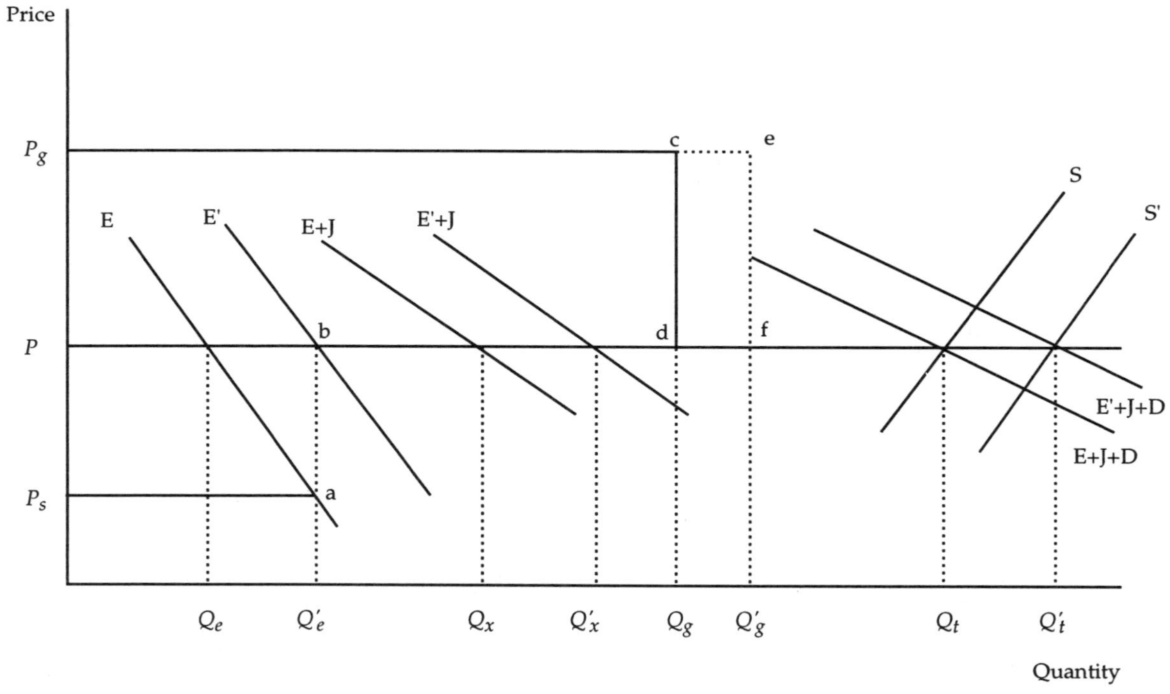

the context of a given deficiency payment program. The program is based on the acreage flexibility features of the 1990 farm act and the frozen payment yields of the 1985 act and may be treated as roughly decoupled. That is, the amount of government deficiency payments has relatively little effect on production, and the quantity produced does not affect the quantity eligible for payment. Price support policies are not included in the figures to simplify the illustration and because price supports have become relatively unimportant in U.S. farm programs in recent years.

Constant ARP. In figure 5–1 the market price that applies when the export subsidy program is not used is shown as P. At this price the market clears at quantity Q_t. The market supply curve, S, crosses the total demand curve, labeled $E+J+D$, at price P and quantity Q_t. Three distinct demand curves indicate three distinct markets for U.S. wheat, and their sum composes total demand. The demand curve labeled E represents the export market to which the export subsidy is applied. The curve that shows the relationship of market price to quantity demanded when an export subsidy is available in this market is illustrated as E'. The per unit subsidy is measured by $P'-P_s$. The nonsubsidized export market is shown by the distance from E to $E+J$. (J is used to represent this market because Japan is the largest importer not provided with EEP subsidies.) Because the J market demand curve is itself downward sloping, the $E+J$ demand curve (representing total exports) is flatter than the E demand curve. The domestic market, D, is also not eligible for subsidies. The size of this market (about half of total demand) is shown by the distance between the curves labeled $E+J+D$ and $E+J$.

When the export subsidy is provided in market E, the resulting total demand is represented by $E'+J+D$, the new market clearing price is P', and the new total market quantity is Q'_t. We will now use the figure to trace through the effects of the subsidy on the various market participants. First, consider the market-subsidized export market denoted by the demand curve labeled E. The subsidized buyers now pay P_s rather than their original price P or the new market price P'. This market now buys quantity Q'_e so additional exports in this market (in proportionate terms) are $(Q'_e - Q_e)/Q_e$. The total expenditures on export subsidies are $(P' - P_s)(Q'_e)$ shown by area $P'deP_s$ in figure 5–1.

Total exports before the EEP are indicated by quantity Q_x. The total percentage of increase in exports, the percentage additionality, is $(Q'_x - Q_x)/Q_x$. The nonsubsidized export quantity had been $Q_x - Q_e$ or the distance between demand curve $E+J$ and demand curve E. The shift from quantity $E+J$ to $E'+J$ caused by the subsidy is equal to the quantity shift from E to E'. And because they are not eligible for subsidy, the consumers in the J market face a price increase from P to P'. In response, they buy less than they did before the EEP. In the figure the quantity indicated by $Q'_x - Q_x$ is less than the quantity $Q'_e - Q_e$.

The domestic buyers also receive no subsidy, and they consume less wheat because the price they face is also higher. They lose consumer net benefits in the amount shown by the area *timl*. This area is equal to *fgkj*. The demand curves $E+J$ and $E'+J$ are parallel (as are $E+J+D$ and $E'+J+D$).

The government spends general tax revenue on the domestic farm income subsidy program as well as on export subsidies. The deficiency payment program for wheat is approximated here by an income transfer that provides a variable subsidy per ton on a fixed quantity of output shown by Q_g. Under the current wheat program this quantity would be approximately constant under changes in the export program and is treated as though it were fixed in this analysis.

Initial deficiency payment program budget costs are $(P_g - P)(Q_g)$ shown by the rectangular area $P_g cbP$. After the market price rises to P', deficiency payment program costs fall to $(P_g - P')Q_g$, shown by area $P_g cnP'$. These budget costs are also program transfers to wheat producers. For the program quantity, the higher price that raises market returns to farmers reduces transfers to farmers by the same amount so the effects on farm incomes are offsetting. The loss of program benefits by producers is offset by a gain in market revenue on this quantity. That is, the dollar amount $(P' - P)Q_g$ becomes sales revenue rather than deficiency payments. In addition, producers gain producer surplus in the amount shown by the area *bnmj*, which applies to the quantity not covered by the deficiency payment program. But while taxpayers gain, consumers lose from higher prices, and some of those losses apply to domestic consumers.

We are now in a position to evaluate the national effects of the export subsidy under the condition that domestic prices rise and farm program payments decline. First consider producers and consumers. As we have just noted, producers gain the area $P' - P$ from Q_g to the supply curve S. Domestic consumer losses are *timl*, which are larger than what producers gain. Taxpayers spend less on domestic subsidy but now have expenditures on the export subsidy.

In the figure the export subsidy outlay is shown by area $P'deP_s$. The upper part of this rectangle $P'doP$ is offset by reduced deficiency payments; the new outlays are $(P - P_s)Q'_e$, shown by area $PoeP_s$. Whether the export program increases or reduces total government outlays depends on the calculation $[(P - P_s)Q'_e] - [(P'-P)(Q_g - Q'_e)]$. In the figure we compare area $PoeP_s$ to *dnbo*. Given the preexisting and constant deficiency payment program, the export subsidy has the potential to reduce the total outlays and taxpayer burden.

A potential benefit of allowing the market price to rise when the subsidy is provided to only a part of the export market is additional revenues to the domestic suppliers from the nonsubsidized export buyers. These revenues have already been included in the additional producer benefits or in the reduced deficiency payments. In the figure, area *ditr* shows the additional revenue earned from foreign buyers that do not benefit from the export subsidy. In our case the reduced deficiency payment associated with this area is not included in the export subsidy outlay or lost domestic consumer outlays.

Constant price. Figure 5–2 illustrates a case for which the acreage allowed for planting under the wheat program increases when the export subsidy program expands export sales. For figure 5–2 the quantity produced expands enough such that the market price is a constant. This is the opposite polar case from the previous illustration of no supply shift. It is illustrated to map the two bounds of the potential domestic policy reaction to export subsidies.

In figure 5–2 export sales in the subsidized market expand from Q_e to Q'_e, and because quantity supplied increases by the same amount, from Q_t to Q'_t, the market price does not rise. The domestic price to consumers does not increase, and the market price to the nonsubsidized export markets also does not increase. In this case there are no budget savings in the domestic farm program to offset export subsidy costs, and farm program payments increase because the production eligible for payments increases as the ARP is reduced.

When the farm price does not rise with more subsidized exports, farmers gain from a relaxation in the requirement to idle land and from additional direct government payments that are made on about two-thirds of the increased production. From a national perspective the economy gains from bringing idled land back into production but loses from subsidies paid to foreigners and from higher taxes or increased budget deficits to finance the export subsidies and the additional deficiency payments to farmers.

TABLE 5-2
EFFECTS OF A TARGETED EXPORT SUBSIDY PROGRAM FOR WHEAT

	Subsidized Exports	Other Exports	Domestic Market	Total Supply	Farm Payments	Export Payments	Total Payments
Farm price				*Dollars per Ton*			
Without subsidy	110.0	110.0	110.0	110.0	36.8	0.0	—
Fixed ARP (1)	80.0	120.0	120.0	120.0	26.8	40.0	—
Fixed ARP (2)	87.6	127.6	127.6	127.6	19.2	40.0	—
Fixed price (1)	70.0	110.0	110.0	110.0	36.8	40.0	—
Fixed price (2)	70.0	110.0	110.0	110.0	36.8	40.0	—
Quantity				*Million Metric Tons*			
Without subsidy	15.0	13.0	34.0	62.0	44.0	0.0	—
Fixed ARP (1)	21.0	12.0	33.0	66.0	44.0	21.0	—
Fixed ARP (2)	24.2	12.0	33.0	69.2	44.0	24.2	—
Fixed price (1)	23.0	13.0	34.0	70.0	49.6	23.0	—
Fixed price (2)	31.4	13.0	34.0	78.4	55.5	31.4	—

Millions of Dollars

Revenue and outlays						
Without subsidy	1,650	1,430	3,740	6,820	1,620	0	1620
Fixed ARP (1)	1,680	1,440	3,960	7,920	1,180	840	2020
Fixed ARP (2)	3,088	1,531	4,198	8,817	845	968	1,813
Fixed price (1)	2,530	1,430	3,740	7,700	1,825	920	2,745
Fixed price (2)	3,454	1,430	3,740	8,624	2,042	1,256	3,298

	(1)	(2)
Export demand subsidized	-1.47	-3.0
Export demand nonsubsidized markets	-0.86	-0.5
Domestic demand	-0.32	-0.2

—. Not applicable.

NOTE: For the entries with an export subsidy, the fixed ARP rows refer to the cases under which the supply function does not shift when the export subsidy is introduced. The fixed price rows refer to the cases under which the supply curve shifts to accommodate the demand increase at a constant domestic supply price. Supply elasticity is 0.71, and the alternative demand parameters are as follows:

SOURCE: Author's construction.

Figures 5–1 and 5–2 have provided two views of how increased export subsidies may be accommodated by the markets and U.S. domestic farm payment programs. It is not clear which of the two approaches most closely reflects the reality of policy interaction. In its budget calculations the Congressional Budget Office tends to assume that the acreage reduction programs are relaxed to accommodate increased export subsidies so that budget costs rise when the EEP increases. Conversely, the Office of Management and Budget, a part of the Executive Office of the President, has assumed that the budget costs of the EEP program have been generally offset by lower deficiency payments because the farm price of wheat rises with the EEP.

We now turn to a more quantitative illustration of the impacts of targeted export subsidies, again under these alternative approaches to program interaction.

A Quantitative Assessment of Targeted Export Subsidies. Now let us attempt to assess quantitatively the net effects of the targeted export subsidy. We can use the figures as a guide, along with some illustrative numbers that correspond roughly to the recent U.S. experience for wheat. Discussion of econometric analysis applied to U.S. wheat trade is provided in Abbott (1988), Blandford (1988), Bredahl et al. (1979), Devadoss and Meyers (1990), Gardiner and Carter (1988), Grennes et al. (1978), Thursby and Thursby (1990), and Veeman (1987). A review of supply and demand parameters can be found in Sumner, Alston, and Gray (1994).

Approximate magnitudes for various prices, quantities and revenues, and effects of the EEP program for wheat are provided in table 5–2. The numbers in the table are provided for illustration and are not based on a comprehensive quantitative analysis applied to current EEP operations. The price and quantity magnitudes listed under the rows for export subsidy case 1 with a constant

ARP, however, do reflect the approximate state of the EEP program in 1993–1994.

In table 5–2 the first row in each panel applies to the case with no export subsidy. In row 1 the market price is $110 per ton; outlays on deficiency payments are $36.80 per ton. In the next two panels the deficiency payments apply initially to 44 million tons eligible for payments and total $1,620 million. In the first quantity row, without the export subsidy, the domestic market is larger than the total export market, and deficiency payments cover somewhat more than two-thirds of the total supply.

Four cases are used to reflect the potential effects of the targeted export subsidy. Two sets of demand elasticity parameters (labeled 1 and 2) are used to reflect our uncertainty about the demand responsiveness, especially in the export markets. In addition, as discussed above, two alternative assumptions about how the acreage reduction program responds to export subsidies are used. In each case the per unit export subsidy is $40 per ton.

As in figures 5–1 and 5–2, farm program payments are made on only a part of production. When the supply function is held fixed as the export subsidy is introduced (fixed ARP), the quantity of production eligible for farm program payments is also held constant at 44 million tons. For these cases the price used for deficiency payment calculations varies from $110 to $127.6 per ton. When the ARP is relaxed and the market price is held constant as the export subsidy is introduced, the quantity eligible for deficiency payments increases. For these cases the share of production eligible for payments remains constant at approximately 71 percent, the same share as used in the base case with no export subsidy.

Parameters. Key parameters used to determine the reactions to the EEP are the demand elasticities in each market and the total U.S. supply elasticity. Case 1 was chosen to reflect recent quantities and prices and an additionality that is consistent with recent estimates. Case

2 parameters were selected to provide larger EEP export gains and large domestic price gains so that there would be a significant potential for total budget savings. In each case attention is paid to the features of the individual markets and recent empirical analysis.

The U.S. EEP program is applied such that demand in much of the nonsubsidized export market is relatively inelastic. The most competitive and price-sensitive markets receive a subsidy; others do not. In particular the Japanese market is known to show relatively little reaction to the export price. In several of the non-EEP markets in South America, the United States is the only export supplier and faces a relatively inelastic demand. In several non-EEP markets, however, suppliers such as Canada, Australia, and Argentina compete with the United States and domestic suppliers, and so the export demand facing the United States is likely more elastic. Based on these considerations, for parameter set 1 the implied export demand elasticity in the nonsubsidized export market is about -0.86. For parameter set 2, the nonsubsidized export market, I use a more inelastic demand elasticity of -0.5. The subsidized export market is substantially more price responsive than the nonsubsidized market. In the subsidized export market, case 1 applies a demand elasticity of -1.47, and case 2 applies a demand elasticity of -3.0.

Domestic demand for U.S. wheat is usually assumed to be quite inelastic in both cases. Most elasticity estimates for domestic demand for wheat for food uses in the United States are in the range of -0.2. Imports remain small in the domestic market, and feed wheat represents less than 20 percent of domestic demand in most years. In case 1, I use a domestic demand elasticity of -0.32. In case 2, I use an inelastic demand elasticity of -0.2 facing U.S. wheat in the U.S. market.

The domestic supply elasticity for wheat, with the ARP constant, depends on the length of run considered and the range of price movements expected. Burt and

Worthington (1991) and the literature reviewed in Sumner, Alston, and Gray (1994) indicate that a supply elasticity of between 0.5 and about 1.0 is a reasonable estimate for moderate supply price changes and a length of run of a few years. For both sets of demand elasticities, I use a supply elasticity of 0.71 to reflect movements along the constant ARP supply curve.

Effects of an export subsidy with a constant ARP. When the ARP is held constant, the domestic price increases along a fixed supply curve, as illustrated in figure 5–1. For parameter set 1, the $40 export subsidy allows the net price to the subsidized market to fall to $80 per ton. Quantity demanded in this market increases from 15 million tons to 21 million tons (40 percent). At the same time the prices facing producers and consumers in the other markets rise by $10 per ton, to $120 per ton. After small declines in the quantity demanded in the nonsubsidized export market, total exports are up by 5 million tons, or about 18 percent. The total quantity demanded (including in the domestic market) is up by 4 million tons, or about 6 percent.

Producers receive a higher price for a larger quantity and receive less in direct transfers through deficiency payments. Total revenue for producers rises from $8,440 million to $9,100 million. Outlays for the export subsidy are shown in the table as $840 million based on a subsidy of $40 per ton for 21 million tons. Outlays for deficiency payments decline substantially under the export subsidy program; the payment rate falls by $10 per ton—more than 25 percent. (The decline is from about $1.00 per bushel to about $0.73 per bushel.) The decline of $440 million in deficiency payments, however, is more than offset by the increase in export subsidy payments. Total outlays increase by $400 million.

The second set of demand elasticities was chosen to be more favorable to the export subsidy program. With parameter set 2, the export demand in the subsidized market is more elastic, and the demands in the nonsubsidized export market and the domestic market are more inelastic than with parameter set 1. Thus subsidized exports expand by more, and the domestic price rises by more with the same $40 per ton export subsidy. Under this parameter set, deficiency payments now decline by almost half when the export subsidy is applied. Export subsidy payments are larger in this case because the tonnage exported with subsidy increases by 9.2 million tons rather than 6 million tons. Total sales revenue is substantially higher under the export subsidy in this case because the market prices are all higher and total supply is larger.

Deficiency payment savings depend on the domestic price impact of the export subsidy and on the quantity eligible for payments. Since the 1990 farm bill, no more than about 70 percent of wheat production is ever likely to be eligible for payments. The payment area is at most 85 percent of the base, and participation is unlikely to exceed the 87 percent reached last year with a zero acreage reduction requirement. Also, payment yields are frozen at the average of actual yields experienced more than a decade ago.

With demand parameter set 1, an export subsidy of $40 per ton applies to 21 million tons. Both these figures and the export subsidy cost of $840 million are consistent with recent data. The average EEP bonus for wheat has been below $40 in some periods and averaged as high as $60 recently. A $10 per ton increase in the domestic price, which is used in the deficiency payment calculations, could be caused by a smaller price per unit export bonus, but that situation would mean a much more elastic response in the subsidized export market or an extremely inelastic supply curve for wheat.

Even in case 2 with a more elastic demand for subsidized exports and inelastic demand in the other markets, the export subsidy program causes a net increase in government outlays. The added exports fail to raise the domestic price enough such that the reduction in deficiency payments offsets the EEP outlays.

The first step in analyzing the budget consequences of the EEP was to ask if total outlays are likely to be reduced. The more elastic the demand in the subsidized market, the more the total demand is shifted out per dollar of subsidy. For a given additionality in the subsidized markets, total quantity demanded increases by more when demand in the nonsubsidized export and domestic markets is more inelastic. On the supply side, the more inelastic is the domestic supply function, the more increases in total demand translate into a price increase rather than an increase in production. It is this domestic price increase that reduces outlays for deficiency payments.

The analysis of the EEP at the Department of Agriculture has often claimed budget neutrality for the EEP (for example, see Salathe [1988] and Gardner [1994]). The USDA has tended to assume high export additionality but also an inelastic supply of wheat and thus an extremely large impact of the export subsidy on the domestic price. One implication of an extremely inelastic supply is that as the domestic price rises, a larger export subsidy is required before a significant net subsidy can be offered. If domestic price increases by $20 per ton, for example, an export bonus of $40 per ton generates only a $20 per ton net decrease in the price for subsidized buyers. With this relatively small net subsidy, an extremely elastic demand response is required to cause a substantial demand shift in total demand facing the U.S. market. Finally, the parameters that allow a budget savings to be projected also imply large costs to domestic consumers. A domestic price increase of $20 per ton in our example would generate savings of $880 million in deficiency payments, leaving payments of only $740 million. In this extreme case the export program implies budget savings of $100 million. The costs of these budget savings, however, would be extremely large additional expenditures by domestic consumers, a large loss in domestic consumer welfare, and a large transfer to foreign buyers.

Administrative costs are another part of the contribution of the export subsidy program to total government budget outlays. Because it does not replace another program, the EEP adds to the total administrative outlays of the USDA. These costs, while not negligible, are likely small, particularly relative to the value of the subsidy and to the budget costs of the farm program. The EEP requires only a small central staff of analysts. The program requires no more than 100 person-years of effort at approximately $100,000 per person. This administrative cost of $10 million amounts to about $0.50 per ton but does not include the costs incurred by export firms in applying for bonuses and complying with the program rules.

Government budget costs of farm programs are a particular concern for two reasons. First, from the practical perspective of the farm constituency, the total outlays available for farm subsidies are almost surely limited. Therefore, if a combination of programs can accomplish additional farmer benefit with the same or lower government outlays, farmers would prefer that situation. Second, taxation itself has costs to the economy. So long as consumer costs are not increased, if the outlay of tax money can be reduced for the same income transfer to farmers the total economic benefit may be increased. Estimates of the deadweight costs of taxation (the excess burden) vary widely, but these costs are likely in the range of 10 to 30 percent (Alston and Hurd 1990; Fullerton 1991). Recognizing the deadweight cost of taxation, if a targeted export subsidy that reduces deficiency payments by more than the amount of the export bonuses can be devised, the whole economy may benefit. Unfortunately, the estimates presented above suggest that such a program does not seem likely under realistic market and program parameters.

Besides the potential to reduce the budget costs of the deficiency payment program, targeted export subsidies may be used to extract economic gains from the nonsubsidized export market through the effects of terms of trade. These gains, however, are quite limited when realistic supply and demand parameters are used. The net terms of the trade benefit of the targeted export subsidy may be indicated by comparing the export subsidy cost with the increase in net export revenues from the nonsubsidized market. In the fixed ARP rows of table 5–2 with demand parameter set 1, the price is up by $10 per ton for 12 million tons for $120 million, but the quantity also falls by 1 million tons so the small loss of profit on this quantity must be subtracted. To earn this increased revenue from nonsubsidized foreigners requires an export subsidy of $840 million and an increase in total government outlays of $400 million. For parameter set 2, the price in the nonsubsidized market increases by $17.60 per ton for 12 million tons for $211 million, and there is a loss of profits on the reduction of sales of about 1 million tons. In this case EEP outlays are $968 million, and the increase in total outlays on the EEP and deficiency payments is about $193 million.

An accounting of net national income effects involves subtracting taxpayer and domestic consumer costs from producer gains. For parameter set 1, the producer surplus gain from a higher price is $200 million, the loss in consumer surplus in the domestic market is approximately $325 million, and the net additional cost to taxpayers from the EEP payments and lower deficiency payments is $400 million. The net effect is a cost to the economy of $525 million. If we estimate the excess burden of taxation at about 15 percent, the added net economic cost of the new outlays is $60 million, and the total loss is $585 million. Using demand parameter set 2 reduces but does not eliminate this net cost to the economy. In this case farmers gain $379 million, consumers lose

$570 million, and net government outlays increase by $193 million. Without recognizing the deadweight cost of taxation, the EEP costs the economy $384 million; if the 15 percent deadweight cost of $29 million is added to the net outlays, the net loss for the economy is $413 million.

Endogenous ARP with constant market price. The second set of assumptions about supply policy and price effects of the EEP is applied next. In this case the ARP for wheat is reduced in response to the export subsidy program such that the price in the U.S. market is no higher than it would be without the export subsidy. There are now no potential budget savings or terms of trade gains from the export subsidy. Farmers, however, gain from much larger quantities produced and sold. In the fixed price rows of table 5–2, the domestic market price remains $110 per ton, and the subsidized export price falls to $70 per ton. In this case, only the demand elasticity in the subsidized export market matters. With the demand elasticity of -1.47, exports rise from 15 million to 23 million tons, and with a demand elasticity of -3.0, the exports rise to 31.4 million tons, and production increases by 16.4 million tons, to 78.4 million tons.

In this case there are no terms of trade gains, and deficiency payments rise rather than fall. The total cost of the domestic payments and the export subsidy program increase to $3,298 million, compared with $1,620 million without the EEP. Partially offsetting these costs is an increase in the productive use of farm land. By reducing the amount of idled acreage, the export subsidy program reduces one economic cost of the domestic wheat program.

A few sample calculations suggest the order of magnitude of this land use effect. Assume first that the value per year of the idled acreage is about $40 per acre and about 15 million acres would be returned to production. With those figures, the value of the land returned to production would be approximately $600 million. The $40 per acre figure is based on an approximate average rental rate of wheat land that would be idled if the ARP were raised. The 15 million acres is based on the amount of land used to produce 16.4 million tons at slightly below average yield per acre.

The $600 million figure is likely an overstatement of the value to the economy of keeping wheat land in production for two major reasons. First, it is difficult to associate 15 million additional wheat acres with the EEP program and in particular with a reduction in the ARP—a figure contrary to the trend for all other commodities. This figure would imply that without the EEP there would have been a 20 to 25 percent wheat ARP in recent years. Second, wheat land has some value when it is idled, and this land is naturally of lower than average productivity. Therefore the $40 per acre rental value probably overstates the value of keeping idled land in production.

In this case an assessment of the EEP for wheat requires comparing the value of using rather than idling additional acreage with the economic cost of transferring tax revenue to foreign wheat buyers. The gain of at most $600 million per year compares with a budget cost of $1,256 million, with a demand elasticity of -3.0. The net losses are even larger if the deadweight cost of taxation is added to the direct budget outlay of the EEP bonuses. In the case for which land is brought into production to supply the additional exports, the net economic cost of the wheat program is approximately $650 million.

Summary and Policy Implications of Export Price Subsidies. The foregoing analysis, focusing particularly on the export enhancement program for wheat, has provided an extensive discussion of the export subsidy programs. The details of the analysis would differ for an analysis of export subsidies for other commodities, but the policy conclusions would not differ. For a number of commodities to which the export subsidies are applied, there are no deficiency payments to be offset. Further, for some commodities, almost all exports are shipped with a subsidy, the United States is a relatively minor player in the world market, or exports play a minor role in total demand for the product. For these commodities it is hard to derive any case in which export subsidies have even the potential to increase national income.

The policy implication from the analysis presented here is that export subsidies are counterproductive as trade policy for U.S. agriculture. Export subsidies as they are currently operated do provide benefits to specific farm interests, but they do so at a large cost to the economy. Further, larger benefits could be delivered to farmers from the smaller budget and economic costs if export subsidies were not used. We should not be fooled by the conceptual possibility that export subsidies could be part of a policy mixture that maximizes benefits to farmers for a fixed economic cost. Such a policy mixture has never been the issue. Export subsidies have been rationalized on purely fallacious, mercantilist grounds.

Export Credit Programs

As with explicit export price subsidies, the United States has a long history of government participation in the supply of credit for the export of farm commodities. Credit subsidies for agricultural exports began decades ago with direct credit for export sales offered by the CCC. Initially credit subsidies were limited to commodities exported from CCC inventories, but for many years they have also been used to finance commercial sales of commodities.

Description of Current Programs. The current export credit programs began in 1980 with the Export Credit Guarantee Program (GSM-102), which provides CCC backing for commercial loans to importers for loans of up to three years. In recent years this program has provided guarantees for about $5 billion of credit per year.

The accompanying Intermediate Export Credit Guarantee Program (GSM-103) is similar but allows loans of three years to ten years. It has had an authorized limit of $1 billion per year (USDA 1991). In recent years about 10 percent of all U.S agricultural exports have been shipped under these credit programs. About 20 to 30 percent of grain and oilseed exports have been financed with credit guarantees, while less than 10 percent of exports of other commodities have used these programs.

U.S. export credit programs are operated as follows. The Department of Agriculture determines eligible countries based on assessments of creditworthiness and potential benefits by commodity. Buyers obtain credit from U.S. commercial banks or other financial institutions, and the export shipper receives cash on shipment. If the foreign buyer fails to repay its loan on schedule, the CCC repays the U.S. financial institution and attempts to collect the repayment directly from the foreign buyer.

Unlike explicit price subsidies, credit programs that meet some basic international criteria are not subject to Uruguay Round GATT disciplines. The understanding during the negotiations was that so long as the explicit subsidy component of credit guarantees was relatively minor and credit was extended with reasonable expectations that it would be repaid, then export credit programs would not be considered as export subsidies. The specific rules limiting the use of credit guarantees were then to be worked out at the OECD in conjunction with the general credit rules for industrial exports. The general expectation is that the agricultural credit programs currently used by the United States will be exempted from export subsidy disciplines under the Uruguay Round agreement and under the forthcoming OECD rules.

Evaluation of Export Credit Guarantee Programs. Credit programs provide export subsidies without direct price subsidization. A number of issues related to export credit programs are similar to those raised by explicit price subsidies (Vercammen and Barichello 1994). These include the effects of credit subsidies on the quantity of exports, on the export and domestic prices, and on the net government farm subsidy budget. In addition, credit subsidies, as implemented by the United States and other major export competitors, are always targeted to particular buyers and therefore have the potential to facilitate price discrimination. Unlike with explicit price subsidies, with credit programs it may be difficult to measure the amount of subsidy provided. Further, the value of the credit guarantee to the buyer may differ from the government cost of the guarantee.

Prior to the Budget Enforcement Act of 1990, Congress and the executive branch used cash accounting to record costs of loan guarantees. Under the budget rules, guarantees were shown as having no cost in the year they were made and might even have shown a small receipt from fees collected. But if a loan went into default, the payment to the commercial bank would be recorded as an outlay, and any subsequent repayments as a receipt at the time they were received.

These rules were changed in 1991. Under current budget rules, the budget costs of credit guarantees are scored as an estimate of the expected value of costs. Consider a $2 billion loan guarantee with a 5 percent chance that the whole value of the loan would not be paid. Under the old rules the expected budget cost of the guarantee was likely to be zero; under the current rules the budget cost is $100 million.

The amount of the implicit export subsidy may be assessed in several ways. One is simply to use the assessment of risks by the government agency under the budget act. For fiscal year 1993, for example, the budget allocation cost originally assigned to GSM-102 and GSM-103 programs and the Emerging Democracies Program, with total program levels of $5.7 billion, was $158.5 million, or 2.78 percent of the budget. Based on the subsequent experiences, the 1993 rate has been revised to 13.2 percent. A larger program level or a more risky portfolio of loans would imply a larger expected budget cost. Currently the executive branch uses an ex ante rate of about 7 percent, and the Congressional Budget Office uses an anticipated loss rate of about 12 percent for agricultural credit guarantees.

The riskiness of a loan may depend in part on the guarantee. The use of U.S. government credit guarantees may itself influence the probability of default. Some foreign governments may find it particularly costly to default on loans backed by the U.S. government. The United States may provide various forms of military and development assistance that could be withdrawn or may otherwise be in a position to exercise pressure on an importer through withholding trade concessions or other benefits. In these cases a credit guarantee by the U.S. government may be an important factor in the feasibility of the entry of exports into selected markets by making payment more likely. Conversely, as with Iraq following the gulf war, sometimes the very fact that loans are backed by the U.S. government encourages default. Care must be taken in using the potential default costs to the U.S. government as an assessment of the benefit of credit guarantees to the importer.

Another measure of the subsidy component of credit guarantees is how much lower the interest rates for the credit extended would have been if the CCC had not provided the guarantees. Under the GSM programs the foreign buyer borrows enough from U.S. banks to make a specific commodity purchase from a U.S. supplier. If one could establish what the terms of the loan would have been with and without the guarantee, one could establish the value of the subsidy. Finally, sales that are not made on a credit basis could be made on a cash basis at a somewhat lower price. An importing country may have the option to purchase a commodity without guaranteed credit. Data on the prices applied in similar transactions made for cash versus those based on guaranteed credit provide another assessment of the value of the export credit guarantee as the equivalent of a price subsidy. There is no reason to expect that these three measures would yield equal measures of subsidy. Nor is it evident which is more appropriate for policy analysis. In fact, there is reason to expect all these measures to be of use if available.

It is possible to use the government budget numbers cited above to calculate some effects of credit guarantees. Let us use the current ex ante estimate of 7 percent of the loaned funds as an approximation of the net value of credit guarantees to compare these subsidies with the EEP. Clearly, with a budget of $1.2 billion for 1993, the EEP was much larger than the export credit programs in terms of total subsidy. Seven percent of $5.7 billion is about $400 million. In 1993 the average EEP bonus was approximately $40 per ton for wheat. Let us examine the subsidies from credit guarantees on a per ton basis. For purposes of comparison, consider the counterfactual experiment in which the credit guarantee program levels were all applied to grain with an export price of $150 per ton. In this case the $5.7 billion would be spread over 38 million tons. Expected losses of the guaranteed funds of approximately $400 million amounts to an expected budget outlay of approximately $10.50 per ton. In fact, credit guarantees have been available for everything from tobacco to vegetable oil exports, but a significant share of the guarantees are used for grain, and much of the wheat and other products that receive EEP bonuses also receive credit backing.

The measure of $10.50 per ton is not a fully accurate measure of the effect of the credit guarantees on the quantity or value of exports. If it were, one could simply apply the appropriate export demand elasticity to the price subsidy equivalent of credit guarantees to arrive at the impact on exports. Countries that make use of export credit guarantees, however, may place higher than average value on subsidies in that form. Alternatively, so long as the credit guarantee is available, a country may use it even though its risk of default is low and it could have had access to commercial credit at only slightly higher interest rates. That is, the value to the importer may be larger or smaller than the expected cost to the U.S. Treasury.

A Policy for Export Credits. Credit subsidies may become an increasingly used export policy as direct price subsidies are phased down under the Uruguay Round agreement. It is therefore especially important to provide some clear definitions to limit the subsidy component in these programs and to begin to place limits on the quantities subsidized and value of the subsidy.

It is hard to see any legitimate rationale for the widespread use of export credit programs. As demonstrated above for other export subsidies, the net effect on national income is in general negative. In some limited cases, however, government-backed credit guarantees could add to the efficiency of international market transactions. In some cases export buyers are foreign governments that could be heavily influenced by the participation of the U.S government to repay loans for which they might not otherwise qualify. In these limited cases some U. S. government participation in the credit process may be useful. Even in these limited cases, however, this government participation could take the form of a legal commitment to help enforce private contracts rather than a financial commitment to repay the loans.

Application of three policy principles to export credit subsidies would help reform the programs. First, more effort is needed to ensure that they not be used as development assistance or rewards to countries for being political allies of the United States. If there is a strong urge for such programs, they should be authorized through the State Department, and the funds should be explicitly appropriated for those purposes. Using the current programs for both commercial and political purposes confuses the administration of the program and is at best misleading to all those involved. Rules now require borrowers to meet minimum standards of creditworthiness before a credit guarantee is issued and require the programs not be used as development aid or political tools. These rules are useful if they are enforced, but such enforcement is difficult and not applied consistently, as demonstrated by the recent extension of credit guarantees to Russia.

Second, vigilant oversight is needed to ensure that accurate ex ante budget costs of credit guarantees are always recorded in the year in which the loans are issued. U.S. policy regarding credit guarantees was much improved with the change in budget rules in 1990: there is now a better chance that the true cost of credit guarantees will be reflected in the appropriations to these programs. What is needed now is a strong effort to ensure that potential losses are not systematically underestimated. If accurate estimates are used, considerable budget pressure will be brought to bear on the credit programs.

Third, export credit guarantees and other potential credit programs should be explicitly acknowledged as export subsidies. Then, with this acknowledgement, the United States should take the lead in including credit subsidies in export subsidy disciplines in multilateral trade agreements. One way to make such an approach politically feasible is for the United States to begin a unilateral reduction of credit guarantees for agricultural exports.

Export Market Promotion

Market promotion programs subsidize activities such as in-store displays, advertising, and participation in international trade shows. Also included in this general classification might be the provision of government personnel and facilities at overseas locations to help firms deal with potential foreign buyers. The United States substantially increased these activities after the 1985 farm bill, but in the past few years these budgets have been somewhat cut back. Unlike many domestic farm subsidy programs, these programs generally are not authorized as entitlements, and funds must be made available for their operation through annual appropriations.

Description of Current Export Market Promotion Programs. The headline case is the Market Promotion Program, which was renamed from the Targeted Export Assistance Program (TEA) in 1990. Other older but smaller USDA programs, such as the Foreign Market Development Program, also provide promotion funding and assistance for food and other agricultural exports. The MPP was originally funded at $200 million per year (the authorized maximum) to provide matching funds for overseas advertising and related promotion activities. After being cut in each of the previous two years, in the fiscal 1995 agriculture appropriations act MPP funding was reduced further to $85.5 million.

Under the MPP the USDA distributes funds to a wide variety of private firms and commodity organizations that complete a complex application process and are willing to submit to detailed program rules and oversight. Diverse activities are funded in numerous countries under the MPP, although some priority is placed on promotion activities that counter unfair trade practices. This money has been used for both branded goods of large multinational firms and for generic promotions by industry organizations. Over the life of the MPP, a substantial share of the funding has been provided to organizations promoting fruits, vegetables, tree nuts, and other high-value per unit and value-added products. This is in sharp contrast to EEP, export credit guarantees, and food aid, which focus primarily on grains and oilseeds.

The Role of Export Market Promotion Assistance. Plausible rationales for export promotion efforts are difficult to find: they are simply handouts to politically favored constituents. Nonetheless, three related hypotheses are examined for why the use of taxpayers funds for overseas advertising serves any general public purpose.

The first concerns some general barriers or market failures that cause firms to underspend on promotion overseas. If marketing firms systematically fail to spend enough on promotion, the rate of return to such investments will remain high, and some encouragement for more spending would seem appropriate. But if firms already spend enough on overseas promotion such that the rate of return on additional promotion is no higher than other investments, then subsidizing these activities will simply cause promotion to be undertaken in excess of the optimal amount. Returns to promotion are notoriously hard to measure, but on the face of it there seems little reason to think that private firms would underinvest and thereby systematically leave profitable opportunities unexploited.

The second hypothesis is that marketing firms may appropriately spend on overseas advertising for benefits that accrue to the firm, but there are external benefits to more export sales that accrue to farms supplying raw materials or to other industries. This argument is that the market system fails to provide exporting firms with the appropriate incentive for export promotions because they do not capture a sufficient share of the benefits. When overseas promotion adds to exports, this added demand for agricultural raw materials benefits farms through more sales at higher prices. Only when the normal market system fails would subsidized promotion return more than the cost to the economy as a whole.

One problem with this hypothesis is that it applies to an equal degree to almost all productive economic activity. A firm seldom captures 100 percent of the benefits of a successful investment. Anytime input prices increase or resources are drawn into production there are upstream economic benefits. If this reasoning is taken seriously, it is an argument for government subsidies for just about every investment in the economy.

An argument with some prima facie plausibility relates to promotion that focuses on generic U.S. products produced by industries with many firms that are not able to organize without government support. In this case the promotion, if successful, would improve the market for all U.S. exporters, and no single firm would have the incentive to undertake such an effort. Generic advertising is common in domestic markets, and its payoff is subject to dispute, in part because it is often difficult to attribute significant gains in industry profitability to generic promotion. Even if such promotion is profitable, however, this argument suggests funding of promotion by an industry consortium, not by the general taxpayer.

Export market promotion programs have been particularly controversial in recent years, even though they remain relatively small in terms of total support compared with the other three categories of export programs discussed in this chapter (GAO 1993). The controversy surrounding the MPP has involved several features of the program. These include support for branded product promotion, support for promotions by large proprietary firms, support for promotions by firms with foreign ownership, and support for promotions without a clear demonstration of success. Conversely, the MPP has been credited with particular merit for emphasizing promotions for high-value and value-added products as opposed to bulk commodity sales.

Like the Targeted Export Assistance Program that it replaced, the MPP has distributed a substantial share of its funding to large firms that sell branded high-value products. Large California cooperatives, such as Sunkist for citrus and Blue Diamond for almonds, have been significant recipients of funding over the life of the program. In addition firms such as Pillsbury (owned by a British parent firm) and Gallo have used MPP funding for overseas promotion of branded products (Ackerman and Smith 1990). Criticism of the program because it supports branded products or products of large firms seems based, however vaguely, on the notion that these firms and these products have sufficient incentives to provide their own advertising funds if the payoff is high enough. Further, the argument seems to be that a significant share of the subsidy is retained by manufacturing or marketing firms. Therefore these funds should not be distributed to firms owned by foreigners. If the reason for the program is simply to increase the demand for U.S. farm output, however, supplementing the promotion budgets of large successful firms may be a reasonable course.

Unpublished attempts to provide support for the payoff to market promotion funds by the Foreign Agriculture Service has indicated amazingly high returns to promotion. This work, however, suffers from methodological defects that render the results less than convincing (Dwyer 1994). The major general problem with empirical estimates showing large gains to promotion is the difficulty in isolating the effects of promotion from the myriad of other factors that affect sales. Studies have been unable to attribute export gains to promotion that might more likely be attributed to price changes, market access improvements, or income growth in export markets. Therefore, it is difficult to prove that export promotion programs have even increased exports and even more difficult to justify the expenditures of tax funds on these programs.

Subsidized promotion activities have characteristics similar to credit guarantees. Both amount to paying an export subsidy in the form of a specific input that is often tied to the primary product sales. Export subsidies provided through promotion would generally be less efficient in expanding exports and more complicated to evaluate than direct price subsidies. But they have not been dealt with comprehensively in international trade agreements because, for one thing, most export competitors do not see subsidized export promotion programs as much of a threat. Nonetheless, promotion aids are export subsidies, and the only rationale for not treating them as such in multilateral agreements is the complexity of designing rules to limit their use without banning them outright. This loophole is likely to be exploited in the wake of the Uruguay Round, as made clear by administration commitments during efforts to pass the legislation implementing the Uruguay Round agreement.

International Food Aid

The United States contributes about $2 billion in food aid each year under several programs: more than half of the world's supply of food aid and about 20 percent of the total U.S. international economic assistance. International food aid is authorized under three distinct titles of the Food for Peace, or PL-480, Program; under section 416(b) of the Agricultural Act of 1949; and under the Food for Progress Program of the 1985 Farm Security Act. The Food, Agriculture, Conservation and Trade Act of 1990 made substantial changes to these programs (Smith and Lee 1994).

Description of Current Food Aid Policies. Since 1990, title 1 of PL-480, operated by the USDA, provides mostly concessional aid to stimulate development and encourage the expansion of commercial markets. Title 2 provides humanitarian aid and donations to stimulate economic reforms through private organizations and multilateral programs. Title 3 provides aid to the least developed nations based on criteria for relieving malnutrition. These latter two titles are administered by the Agency for International Development. The amount and form of food donations under section 416 (b) relies on surplus commodities held by the CCC.

The Uruguay Round agreement on export subsidies provides some general criteria for bona fide food aid but does not limit its use. Not only does the Uruguay Round agreement not restrict food aid shipments, it encourages them as a part of the effort to ensure that the agreement does not harm developing countries. As long as U.S. food aid programs continue to meet the criteria of the agreement, they can continue to operate unencumbered.

As commercial exports have expanded and the share of bulk commodities has declined, food aid has also gradually become a smaller share of total U.S. agricultural exports. In recent years total food aid has been worth $1–2 billion out of total agricultural exports of more than $40 billion (Smith and Lee 1994). The recent 1995 budget for PL-480 is about $1.3 billion, down from $1.7 billion two years earlier. Because large CCC grain stocks were reduced in the early 1990s, commodities available for section 416 distribution have been largely eliminated. The commodity allocation of food aid has changed little in recent years, with most aid continuing to be drawn from bulk grains and vegetable oil.

Evaluation of Food Aid Programs and Proposals for Reform. Three arguments for food aid contribute to its use in the United States. The first is humanitarian—providing food to the hungry is simply the decent thing to do when people are in dire circumstances. The second argument is that food aid is a part of long-term development assistance. The benefit for the United States to contribute development assistance is often framed in humanitarian, political, and economic terms. The economic argument for aiding economic development is that as poor countries grow, they become better markets for U.S. exports. The third argument is that food aid provides a fully subsidized market for U.S. farm output. The U.S. government acquires stocks in the context of other programs; food aid is used to distribute the product without disrupting the commercial market.

Food aid represents 2–5 percent of the value of agricultural exports but remains a significant source of export demand for a number of commodities. These include wheat, rice, and dairy products, among a few others. In general the impact of food aid on total agricultural exports is relatively minor by any measure, and even smaller once one recognizes that at least some portion of food aid is at the expense of commercial exports. Given the availability of variable EEP bonuses and export credit guarantees, some form of subsidized commercial sales might have been made in some cases of food aid. No quantitative assessment of the offset of commercial sales by food aid, however, has been attempted here.

Food aid has at best questionable value as development assistance. In many cases an attempt is made to reduce the negative effect on local agricultural production. The distribution of food aid often allows, and may require, the recipient country to distribute the food through concessional local sales rather than through giveaway programs. Depending on how these sales are administered, the recipient government may earn revenue to be used for other development purposes and may minimize the adverse effect on domestic farm producers. Such effects, however, cannot be eliminated.

If aid is successful, it contributes to long-term income growth in developing countries. More income almost surely translates into more demand for U.S. exports, including agricultural exports. Food assistance reduces the returns to investment in agriculture by poor countries. Even if measures are taken to reduce the adverse impact on farming in the recipient countries, the supply of food aid must reduce to some degree the demand for domestic food production compared with the case when aid is provided in cash or in some other form. Food aid tends to lower agriculture production growth as a share of all growth and maintain a market for U.S. exports even after a poor country has graduated to being a commercial customer. It is certainly cynical and probably not practical to support food aid because it reduces the long-term development of agricultural resources in poor countries. Such support is likely to be self-defeating. Aid in general is of questionable value, and food shipments are clearly less effective than untied aid as contributors to economic development. They can be made less flawed only with detailed safeguards. Shipping aid in a form that lowers the potential for a beneficial impact on economic growth lowers the potential for longer-term demand for agricultural imports. Food aid furthers the long-term prospects of food exporters only if the bias against agriculture that it introduces in poor countries more than offsets its detrimental impact on total growth compared with unrestricted aid.

The Uruguay Round agreement on agriculture included no limits on bona fide food aid; it actually envisioned an increase in food aid to offset the anticipated increases in world market grain prices on poor food-importing countries. The U.S. Uruguay Round implementing law states that "the United States should increase its contribution of bona fide food assistance to developing countries consistent with the Agreement on Agriculture" (section 411[e] Food Aid [2] Sense of Congress subparagraph [B]). This nonbinding sense of Congress obviously depends on annual appropriations to have any real force.

The 1990 FACT Act revised the operation of food aid programs under PL-480 by more clearly delineating the division of responsibility between the USDA and AID (USDA 1991). This division is unlikely to be revisited. Annual appropriations determine the funds available for food aid. The 1995 farm bill may have relatively little impact as long as the authority for aid is maintained. One continuing controversy relates to the cargo preference rules that require at least 75 percent of food aid to be transported in U.S. vessels. The cost of shipping using U.S. vessels is more than double that of foreign competitors and the cargo preference adds substantially to the cost of food aid. The implication is that the quantity of food shipped is significantly smaller for the same budget outlay under cargo preference rules. Humanitarian aid under title 2 of PL-480 will continue to be distributed to poor countries during times of stress. Therefore, as other food aid is reduced, cargo preference should be withdrawn from the remaining shipments so that they can do the most humanitarian benefit for the given outlay.

U.S. Export Policy and the Implementation of the Uruguay Round Agreement

In response to the completion of the Uruguay Round and multilateral reductions in export subsidies, the United States determined that it would treat negotiated maximum subsidy limits as minimums. Although the rationales for and effectiveness of export market promotion and credit programs are acknowledged to be questionable, spending for promotion of these programs may actually increase as the Uruguay Round is implemented.

As legislation implementing the draft was being developed, proposals for increased outlays on trade promotion were progressing though Congress. The Agriculture Investment and Market Expansion Program Bill (HR 4675) would have required savings from reduced export price subsidies to be used for domestic and export programs that did not fall under Uruguay Round disciplines. Under this legislation, programs such as the MPP, PL-480 food aid, and export credits under GSM-102 would have expanded to use the dollars released by reduced EEP bonuses. If lower EEP outlays meant increases in deficiency payments, the added expenditures on other export programs would have represented a net increase in the agriculture budget.

The legislation implementing the Uruguay Round does not contain such measures. The administration, however, has made public pledges that it will proceed along these same lines. While the implementing legislation was being considered, the secretary of agriculture and the director of the Office of Management and Budget jointly stated that export subsidies would be continued at the maximum allowable levels for the next six years. They further stated that the administration would propose increasing the funding for domestic and export market promotion programs by $600 million over five years. In addition, they pledged full funding for the Conservation Reserve Program and discretionary farm programs. These pledges were contained in a letter on September 30, 1994, to the chairmen and ranking members of the House and Senate agriculture committees and as such are a significant statement of policy (Espy and Rivlin 1994).

The challenge for the 1995 farm bill is to ensure that the Uruguay Round agreement not lead to more trade distortion rather than less. There is no reason to allow specific industries to use a multilateral agreement as justification for policies that do not contribute to the national welfare.

6
Extending and Improving International Trade Agreements

Agricultural trade policy involves more than unilateral reforms of agricultural policies. Particularly in the wake of the Uruguay Round, the importance of a policy for negotiating continuations and extensions of the current agreements and perhaps new multilateral agreements is obvious. Expanding or deepening the liberalization in international trade agreements is likely to be a valuable enterprise. This activity should be used not to substitute for appropriate unilateral reforms but to extend the scope of liberal trade policy.

The Value of International Negotiations

For many years economists and policy participants have recognized that trade policy pursued on a multilateral basis is particularly valuable. The basis for the GATT, and now the WTO, is that trade policy is an international affair. Empirical economic models also confirm that gains from trade liberalization are larger if trading partners also reform (Tyers and Anderson 1992). But unilateral trade subsidies and barriers are usually not as damaging to the domestic and international economies if they can be pursued without retaliation. In any case, because trade policy is best undertaken in consultation and negotiation with trading partners, therefore a significant part of a nation's trade policy consists of its positions on international negotiations. (See, for example, papers in Anania et al. [1994].)

Trade negotiations use mercantilist rhetoric that refers to allowing import access as a concession and measures trade compensation as an allowance for trade barriers. The same jargon that refers to more exports than imports as a "favorable" trade balance is used in trade negotiations. It may seem surprising therefore that trade agreements actually do reduce import barriers and export subsidies.

There are three sorts of direct economic benefits for the United States from international agreements to liberalize trade policies. First, the United States benefits directly in the international export market when foreign countries have lower import barriers and devote less to subsidize exports. Second, the world economy grows more rapidly with liberalized trading rules. Freer trade is good for economic growth for a number of reasons related to expanded investment and more efficient capital flows as well as more rational production patterns in the world. Further, as models of Uruguay Round benefits indicate, the U.S. economy gains substantially when there is more economic growth among our trade partners. Finally, when part of an international agreement, some trade policy reforms that could not be instituted unilaterally are feasible politically. Therefore international agreements may have an indirect policy benefit in the United States. And as the previous chapters have documented, the U.S. economy gains when U.S. trade policies are liberalized.

Current trade negotiation policies for the United States include establishing positions regarding the extension of NAFTA and the continuation of the Uruguay Round policy reforms now under way. In addition, new ideas for free trade areas, such as in the Asian Pacific Rim, are useful to explore. Further, it is also important to establish policies that make it easier rather than harder to negotiate trade agreements that remove barriers and reduce subsidies. This chapter deals with each of these issues, with primary emphasis on the importance of continuing the multilateral reform process begun with the Uruguay Round agreement.

Extending NAFTA and Expanding Regional Trade Agreements. For NAFTA, continuation and extension mean primarily expanding the number of countries involved. The details about the path and pace of liberalization will be adjusted in bilateral negotiations. But to be consistent with the agreement between the United States and Mexico, agreements with additional countries must lead to the elimination of import barriers.

Extending the agreement to the south has a number of significant benefits to agricultural trade. Probably the most important gain is the increase in economic stability that a NAFTA agreement would provide to Latin American nations. That increased stability translates into increased access to capital, more investment, and faster income growth. And one implication of more income in Latin America is greater demand for agricultural exports from the United States.

Many trade barriers in Latin America have been reduced as a part of the Uruguay Round and, more importantly, as a part of unilateral reforms in most countries of the region. Remaining trade barriers, however, are significant even in some countries with quite open markets generally. Chile, for example, continues to restrict grain imports and protect a few other domestic agricultural industries. Gradually eliminating these barriers would expand the market for U.S. agricultural exports, and faster economic growth in Chile would make it a more valuable market.

One consideration for new NAFTA-like agreements

relates to the extent of participation. Certainly there is no inherent reason to limit bilateral free trade negotiations to the Western Hemisphere. For agriculture, an aggressive free trade effort in Asia might have an even larger payoff. Currently Japan, Korea, and others in Asia continue to restrict agricultural imports with high tariffs and tariff-rate quotas. The extension of NAFTA to Asia could accelerate the Uruguay Round reduction of trade barriers throughout the regions. The late 1994 discussion at the Asia-Pacific summit meeting in Jakarta was encouraging in that at least the goal of a more open trade policy has been accepted by most nations in the region.

Some observers have expressed concerns that regional trade agreements can be used for protectionism rather than for market opening. Regional trade groups may be seen by some as a substitute for more broad international agreements. But such problems can be avoided if care is exercised in establishing trade agreements. In particular no new trade barrier should be erected, and rules with respect to country of origin need to be flexible enough that the effective rates of protection are not raised. Regional trade agreements always increase the relative trade barriers to nonmembers, but they can otherwise provide general benefits. Successful regional trade agreements, for example, increase the rate of economic growth for their members. This added income is good for all participants in the world economy. Also, and perhaps more important, regional trade agreements can help demonstrate the benefits of more open markets generally. Such a demonstration may make it easier to achieve more progress in the continuing multilateral trade negotiation under the new World Trade Organization.

Continuation of Multilateral Reforms

This section considers a variety of issues related to the pace and form of multilateral negotiations for trade liberalization. In one sense this section is a critique of the Uruguay Round with suggestions for what to continue and what to change.

Sanitary and Phytosanitary Regulations. It is difficult to know what more needs to be done in this area until we see how effective the newly negotiated rules are. In particular, as specific disputes are processed through the WTO and international scientific groups such as the Codex Alimentarious, it will become more clear whether countries continue to use food safety, animal health, and plant health claims as excuses for trade barriers with little scientific backing. In general the guidelines negotiated in the Uruguay Round are regarded by the export industries as being as strong as could be expected. The next round of multilateral negotiations on sanitary and phytosanitary issues will naturally be devoted to responding to the unforeseen complications from the rules created in the Uruguay Round.

Import Barriers. The Uruguay Round converted most nontariff barriers to tariffs. Completing the task requires that Japanese and Korean rice quotas become tariff-rate quotas. Allowing these quotas to remain in place until the end of the implementation period facilitated completing the Uruguay Round negotiations, but these exceptions to universal tariffication must be eliminated to prevent other countries from using that status as legitimacy for similar claims. In particular, import protection in the United States is now on the basis of GATT-bound tariffs; it is important to avoid pressure for new nontariff barriers. One of the few heartening features of the new "voluntary" import restrictions on wheat and the authorization for new tobacco barriers in the Uruguay Round agreement implementing legislation was the use of tariff-rate quotas in both cases, rather than pure nontariff barriers.

Among the most trade-distorting results of the Uruguay Round agreement was the extreme height of the new tariff barriers created during the conversion of quotas and variable levies to tariff-rate quotas (Josling and Tangermann 1994). All major participants created tariff-rate quotas with excessive tariffs for the second tier of tariff-rate quotas. It is now appropriate to begin the accelerated reduction of these excessively prohibitive duties even before the end of the current implementation period of six years. Even without convening a new negotiating round, major agricultural trading partners could agree jointly to readjust the duties applied to the overquota imports in the new tariff-rate quotas. The remaining tariffs may still be prohibitively high, but an adjustment would at least reduce the number of years before some trade would occur. This policy would "simply" entail multilateral agreement by major participants that they would simultaneously revise their most protectionist tariff-rate quotas.

The Uruguay Round agreement provided for an average tariff reduction of 36 percent by tariff line with a 15 percent minimum reduction over a six-year period. Products with the most political sensitivity are likely to be on the list for the minimum rate of reduction. By the year 2001 the tariff rates for these products will remain at 85 percent of the rates at the start of the implementation period. To achieve a 36 percent average, tariffs on many products were reduced at a rate of more than 36 percent, and some tariffs removed altogether. In the next round it is important to accelerate the rate of reduction in tariffs. If an average of 6 percent per year from the initial base period rates could be maintained, agricultural trade barriers would be eliminated by the year 2012—seventeen years from the beginning of the implementation period. No matter how high the initial tariffs were, they could be brought to zero in a relatively short period of time even if a fairly moderate pace were maintained.

The United States could facilitate multilateral reform

by supporting a continuation of agricultural tariff reductions at an accelerated pace after the current implementation period has run its course. With the goal of continuing to reduce trade agricultural tariffs toward zero, the specifics of the pace are less important than the clear signal that no slowing of progress is acceptable.

Export Programs. The Uruguay Round sent mixed signals about export subsidies. Export subsidies remain explicitly outlawed in manufacturing and other areas of commerce. In agriculture, however, export subsides now have official status as accepted policy tools. Further, export promotion assistance, credit subsidies, and food aid are outside even the modest limits placed on explicit export price subsidies. Conversely, compared with the subsidization that has been undertaken in the past decade, the mandated reductions in both the quantities subsidized and the subsidy outlays are significant. No new commodities may be added to those with export subsidies, and for those commodities with large subsidy increases during the 1990s, a major reduction in subsidy is required. For commodities such as wheat, which have been the subject of a continual subsidy battle, the boost to world prices and the added market opportunities for nonsubsidized exporters are a major quantitative benefit of the Uruguay Round agreement.

For explicit export price subsidies (such as the EEP), the 21 percent reduction in the quantity subsidized is likely to have the most binding effect in the next few years (USDA 1994b). The reduction by 36 percent in the value of export subsidy, however, may be the most significant restriction in the long term if the pace of reform is continued. Further, as some U.S. industries and politicians continue to point out, the value of European Community export subsidies remains far larger than those offered by the United States. That value gap will narrow progressively over time as subsidies are reduced. U.S. export industries will benefit significantly if the pace set by the Uruguay Round agreement is maintained or accelerated.

For export credit subsidies and marketing assistance, tight criteria that limit the implicit or explicit subsidy component are not yet included in the international rules. As direct price subsidies become more restricted, more international attention to these indirect export subsidies is likely. The challenge is to undertake multilateral negotiations among major trading partners to limit the use of credit and marketing subsidies as substitutes for price subsidies without becoming bogged down in complex and unenforceable rules.

Because issues about the size of the indirect subsidy element require further analysis, negotiation in these areas is difficult. Setting limits on the total outlays for credit subsidies, the total value of exports for which credit is subsidized, or some similar index may be useful. For marketing assistance, the activities that are subsidized by the government might be limited. Alternatively outlays on marketing assistance could simply be included in the export subsidy total and reduced accordingly.

Two implications are important for the 1995 farm bill and continuing negotiations. First, the United States should begin the accelerated unilateral reduction in export price subsidies so that achieving reduced subsidies multilaterally would be that much easier. If the United States proceeded with subsidy cuts ahead of schedule, we would be in a strong position to demand that others follow. Second, the United States should take the lead in urging that nonprice export subsidies be included in WTO disciplines on export subsidies. The best way to do this is by continuing to reduce these programs unilaterally.

If they were ever important, the time for U.S. export subsidy programs to be trade policy weapons is now past. The United States has substantial negotiating clout in multilateral negotiations because of the size of our national economy. In most cases we can trade better market access for trade benefits without using an export subsidy war that damages us more than our trade competitors.

Internal Supports. The Uruguay Round negotiations spent more rhetoric and more pages of text on internal supports than on any other category. Much of the debate dealt with using an aggregate measure of support (AMS) to summarize policies to be reformed. (For background on the AMS, see IATRC [1990], OECD [1991], and USDA [1989].) This was also the category for which the positions of the negotiating parties changed most over the course of the negotiations. When the debate on internal supports began in earnest in 1991, it quickly became clear that, at the level of reductions considered feasible, the United States would not be required to make any substantial reductions in the programs for major commodities. U.S. reforms undertaken during the 1980s and early 1990s for purely internal reasons, in response to domestic political and budget pressures, fully satisfied the internal support commitments contemplated. Further, once the EU began moving toward a CAP reform proposal to implement direct payment programs, which would become similar to those used in the United States, it was obvious that the Uruguay Round agreement would apply no binding internal support commitments except perhaps on a few minor commodities or some minor traders.

Even in the Dunkel Draft Final Act in 1991—submitted by the GATT chairman to break an impasse in the Uruguay Round negotiations—the required changes in domestic subsidies were minimal (Sumner 1992). This was particularly true because all major participants, such as the United States, the EU, Japan, Canada, and the Nordic countries, favored excluding from discipline various popular policies that use environmental programs, crop insurance, disaster assistance, or regional support as a justification for subsidies. By the time of the Blair House Accord of 1992, what was left of the internal support disciplines was pure window dressing—elaborate window dressing, but transparently nothing of substance.

Dropping any effective disciplines on internal supports from the package was the final step in the progression of internal supports from the center of the negotiations to the periphery. As negotiations continued, it became clear that trying to create disciplines on internal support policies would be inordinately complicated and fraught with problems—policies having similar trade effects would be treated differently; programs with different trade effects would be treated as though they were similar; and loopholes would cause continuing domestic policies to become more trade distorting rather than less. Further, when alternative schemes for reduction of distortions were analyzed quantitatively, it became clear that most of the measurable effects of distortions on international trade were due to border measures and especially to export subsidy programs (see Sumner [1993 and 1994] and USDA [1992]). In practice even tight limits on internal support policies would be likely to have small effects on trade.

There are number of additional reasons to focus trade agreements on border measures rather than on internal support measures.

• Internal subsidy programs are impossibly complex to incorporate effectively into trade agreements. There will be loopholes, and therefore the disciplines will be ineffective. Political effort, popular sentiment, and the scarce effort of negotiators will be wasted. Further, inevitable mistakes in developing an agreement make it likely that in some cases more distorting policies would replace relatively benign policies.

• Reducing trade barriers and export subsidies makes trade-distorting internal subsidy programs much harder for a government to sustain. These policies either are expensive or depend on border measures. Therefore, with less border distortion they tend to decline even if specific multilateral restraints are not applied.

• Internal subsidies are themselves mostly ineffective to constrain imports or expand exports without the accompanying border measures. This is all the more true when countervailing duties, antidumping provisions, and nullification and impairment provisions and procedures in international agreements are available. In the Uruguay Round the internal subsidies were provided with multilateral justification, and the peace clause protects protectionist domestic policies.

• The inclusion of internal subsidies in an agreement makes it harder to apply nullification and impairment or other measures and thus may weaken current remedies. At the worst, because of including internal support disciplines in the GATT, trade may become more restricted than before the agreement.

• Finally, internal supports for agriculture tend to be politically popular. Reducing internal support to satisfy the demands from a nation's trade competitors makes trade agreements more vulnerable and harder to negotiate and implement. Implementation is hard enough without facing the charge that the farm bill is being written in Geneva.

A negotiating position for the next round of multilateral reforms might be simply to let the internal support provisions of the Uruguay Round lapse and to focus all energies on the border measure provisions outlined above.

Peace and Dispute Settlement. If the internal support provisions in the current agreement are allowed to lapse, most of the so-called peace clause is also no longer operative. This may allow more scope for countervailing duty cases and efforts to reduce subsidies through nullification and impairment claims. Trade dispute cases are pursued sometimes to open markets or block export subsidies and sometimes to serve protectionist aims when direct barriers are not available. Countervailing duties and antidumping procedures are in place to discourage countries from subsidizing exports indirectly through domestic subsidies. But admittedly they are often used simply to protect a domestic industry.

The difficulties highlighted above in assessing domestic subsidies are evident in the controversies surrounding countervailing duty cases. Even between such close trade partners as Canada and the United States, it is often not clear whether domestic subsidies have accounted for export success. In the wheat dispute discussed in previous chapters, before pressuring the government to undertake a section 22 case, U.S. wheat interests pursued a number of unfair trade practice cases against Canada and the Canadian Wheat Board. These were not successful, either before the International Trade Commission or a binational dispute panel (U.S.-Canada Binational Panel, [1993] and U.S. ITC [1994b]). In frustration the industry dropped its efforts to prove unfair trade practices and simply lobbied for direct trade barriers. But even in this forum when it was strictly irrelevant, the U.S. wheat industry continued to argue that illegal subsidization accounted for exports of wheat (U.S. ITC 1994a).

This example and a multitude of similar cases suggest that industries that want protection from imports will almost always point to unfair subsidies by their competitors. Strong rules for proof that domestic programs have had a major effect on trade would discourage unsubstantiated claims and would reduce the chance that trade restraints could be erected in response to domestic subsidies in other countries. A somewhat weaker standard might be applied to claims against domestic subsidies that limit imports. In the case of domestic subsidies as an import barrier, the remedy would be to place restrictions on the domestic program itself on an ad hoc basis. The result would be more trade, not less. The recent GATT dispute involving the EU oilseed program is instructive in this regard. Having been found in violation of nullification and impairment of its zero tariff binding for oilseed imports, the EU has reformed its domestic subsidy program for oilseed production. Less EU oilseed output and more access for imports resulted. Thus in this case a domestic program was reformed with no domestic support provisions included in the GATT. Clearly, under the Uruguay Round agreement for internal support, the EU oilseed program would have remained in force and would be continuing to restrict imports.

Conclusions about
Negotiations and Agricultural Trade Policy

International trade negotiations are important but not a substitute for domestic trade policy reforms. Occasionally there are strategic reasons for undertaking policies to negotiate more successfully for multilateral reform. Such an argument, however, is more common as an excuse for protectionism and subsidy to be maintained for their own sake than as a careful quantitative assessment of the national interest. This chapter has urged international negotiations to pursue further trade liberalization on a global basis as soon as possible. But a negotiating position is not a substitute for policy reform that is in the national interest in any case. Therefore, preparing for negotiations should not be used to avoid unilateral reform in the 1995 farm bill.

7
An Agenda for Agricultural Trade Policy

The major criterion for the trade provisions of U.S. farm legislation is the facilitation of continued movement toward multilateral liberalization consistent with the implementation of the Uruguay Round agreement. This direction may be accomplished by policy reforms that bring U.S. agricultural policy more in line with the comprehensive trade policy aims of the United States. Using export subsidies and import barriers to provide income support for farm industries or to insulate domestic farm programs has a long tradition in the United States (Benedict and Stine 1956; Johnson 1950). Having turned the corner on multilateral agricultural trade rules with the Uruguay Round, however, the United States now has the opportunity to make its policy more consistent with its liberal trade rhetoric.

Phase Out Barriers

Simple Tariffs. It is probably too much to expect the 1995 farm bill unilaterally to reduce agricultural tariffs. Such reduction must await new multilateral negotiations. Among the highest or most protectionist of the agricultural tariffs, however, are some associated with new GATT-bound tariff-rate quotas created during the Uruguay Round implementation. Several of these are high by any objective measurement of the internal and border prices on which they were to be based. They are not excessive, however, in comparison with many applied by the Canadians and Europeans. To move toward liberalization, legislation should (1) avoid new tariff barriers, (2) readjust those barriers that are clearly out of line (and punish such exporters as New Zealand and Argentina, which have generally supported liberalization at home and abroad), and (3) provide support wherever possible for renewed early multinational negotiations to reduce the excessive tariff rates set by many nations during the tariffication process.

New tariff-rate quotas. The Canada-U.S. agreement on wheat imports negotiated during the summer of 1994 raises troublesome issues regarding trade policy in the context of NAFTA and the Uruguay Round agreement. What is the value of a free trade agreement or GATT-bound tariffs and World Trade Organization rules when the United States can use threats of unilateral action to coerce "voluntary" trade barriers to be erected? If the United States does not honor its trade agreements, powerful trade partners might understandably hesitate to negotiate with it. The most troublesome aspect of the Canada-U.S. wheat agreement is its contravention of the domestic welfare of the United States. The agreement will do little to change wheat trade and little if anything for the U.S. wheat industry. As is common with such attempts to plug a hole in a trade wall that is structurally unsound, substitute sources of a product—in this case including other grain, pasta, and flour products—will flow around the barrier and offset even the mild restrictions negotiated. The result of this specific instance is symbolic: the United States is an unreliable trade partner that does not honor its commitments. U.S. legislation can contribute by withdrawing the wheat trade barriers and placing limits instead on the ability of negotiators to create similar barriers for other industries.

New trade barriers. The Uruguay Round was to have eliminated nontariff barriers in agriculture. Unfortunately the United States was moving counter to the letter and spirit of the agreement as it was being finalized and implemented. The 1993 law providing for a domestic content scheme for cigarettes created a new nontariff trade barrier for tobacco imports that not only contradicted Uruguay Round reforms but also violated the existing GATT rules. Negotiations under GATT article 28, to arrive at a "voluntary" settlement with affected parties, while legal under GATT, are clearly not consistent with the stated U.S. policy of ridding world agricultural trade of trade barriers. Further, it is questionable that such efforts are even in the long-term self-interest of the U.S. tobacco industry. These new trade barriers should be reversed at the first opportunity; the 1995 farm bill may provide the legislative vehicle. Further, the United States should resist the temptations to create the new trade barriers that will surely be urged by domestic industry interests on occasion. Allowing the trade landscape to become littered by new trade barriers would defeat the purpose of the trade cleanup effort represented by the Uruguay Round.

Phase Out Export Subsidies

The EEP and Related Programs. At the urging of the United States, the Uruguay Round began the movement to phase down export subsidies gradually. The United States pushed for the elimination of the export subsidies even after it had given up on its initial proposal to eliminate multilaterally all farm trade barriers and subsidy programs. Further, one of the few rationales provided for the subsidies that made any economic sense was that the EEP may have been useful to encourage Europe to negotiate seriously in the Uruguay Round. That motivation for export subsidies has now passed. In addition, as domestic commodity programs are reduced, any potential for export subsidies to offset costs of domestic programs is even less important. The United States has more reason unilaterally to eliminate export subsidy programs and less reason to maintain them for complicated strategic or second-best reasons.

It remains true that multilateral subsidy reductions are better than unilateral reductions. That suggests a strategy of attempting to negotiate export subsidy cuts jointly with the European Union and Canada. But the superiority of multilateral reforms is not a reason to ignore the costs of export subsidies to the U.S. economy.

Export Credit and Market Promotion Subsidies. These subsidies are exempt from serious constraint in the Uruguay Round agreement. The resources devoted to these programs was declining recently because of budget pressure and because of a lack of evidence that they increase exports significantly. Then, in the fall of 1994, as a part of the effort to implement the Uruguay Round agreement, these programs gained new support.

Export credit and marketing subsidies should be evaluated for their effect on the national welfare, and such an evaluation would almost surely suggest that they be eliminated. Two exceptions may require further consideration. First, if in the case of commodity sales to foreign governments the involvement of the U.S. government in the credit transaction reduces the risk of default significantly, then some role for government support of U.S. lenders may be useful. The frequency of this case is unclear, however, and the effective role for the government may be simply to provide assistance in contract enforcement. Second, for generic promotion in overseas markets, industry groups may wish to make use of the same kind of checkoff programs now used for domestic promotion.

Such funds are now also used internationally, and their expansion offers an alternative for taxpayer funding.

Food Aid. Food aid programs are export subsidies when they provide commodities to otherwise commercial buyers. As explicit export subsidies are reduced, industries will have an added incentive to lobby for more use of food aid in questionable cases. In some cases the food aid is most likely to reduce incentives for domestic agricultural development in poor countries. Food aid for purely humanitarian purposes will and should continue. For humanitarian programs, cargo preference rules should be dropped so that the most food can be delivered for the limited budget available. Other food aid programs should be reduced for the benefit of taxpayers and domestic consumers as well as agriculture in poor countries.

The 1995 Farm Bill

This book provides information and analysis of agricultural trade policies. It uses this analysis to suggest policy reforms. The general thrust has been in the direction of open and unsubsidized agricultural trade. These reforms were suggested as negotiating positions where progress is possible multilaterally and as unilateral reforms where multilateral implementation would be delayed.

The 1995 farm bill offers the opportunity to reform farm trade policy in the direction that the United States has long claimed was appropriate. That means reversing some recent policies and reinforcing movements toward liberalization wherever the momentum has stalled.

References

Abbott, P. C. "Estimating U.S. Agricultural Export Demand Elasticities: Econometric and Economic Issues." Chapter 3 in *Elasticities in International Agricultural Trade*, edited by C. A. Carter and W. H. Gardiner. Boulder Colo.: Westview Press, 1988.

Abbott, P. C., and P. L. Paarlberg. "Modeling the Impact of the 1980 Grain Embargo." Chapter 11 in *Embargoes, Surplus Disposal, and U.S. Agriculture*. Staff Report AGES860910, U.S. Department of Agriculture, Economic Research Service, November 1986.

Abbott, P. C., P. L. Paarlberg, and J. A. Sharples. "Targeted Agricultural Export Subsidies and Social Welfare." *American Journal of Agricultural Economics* 69 (1987): 723–32.

Ackerman, K. Z., and M. E. Smith. *Agricultural Export Programs*. Washington, D.C. USDA/ERS, Staff Report AGES9033, May 1990.

Alston, J. M. "Economics of Commodity Supply Controls." In *Improving Agricultural Trade Performance under the GATT*, edited by Tilman Becker et al. Kiel: Wissenschaftsverlag Vauk, 1992, pp. 83–103.

Alston, J. M., and B. H. Hurd. "Some Neglected Social Costs of Government Spending in Farm Programs." *American Journal of Agricultural Economics* 72 (February 1990): 149–56.

Alston, J. M., C. A. Carter, R. Gray, and D. A. Sumner. "Domestic Distortions and the Gains from Trade Liberalization: The Case of Canada-U.S. Durum Wheat Trade." Paper presented at the American Agricultural Economics Association annual meeting, San Diego, August 1994.

Alston, J. M., C. A. Carter, and V. H. Smith. "Rationalizing Agricultural Export Subsidies." *American Journal of Agricultural Economics* 75 (November 1993): 1000–9.

Alston, J. M., R. Gray, and D. A. Sumner. "The Wheat War of 1994." *Canadian Journal of Agricultural Economics* 42 (December 1994): 231–51.

Alston, J. M., and D. A. Sumner. "A New Perspective on the Farm Program for U.S. Tobacco." Department of Agricultural Economics, University of California, Davis, 1988.

Anania, G., et al., eds. *Agricultural Trade Conflicts and the GATT: New Dimensions in U.S.-European Agricultural Trade Relations.* Oxford: Westview Press, 1994.

Anania, G., M. Bohman, and C. Carter. "United States Export Subsidies in Wheat: Strategic Trade Policy or Expensive Beggar-Thy-Neighbor Tactic." *American Journal of Agricultural Economics* 74 (1992): 534–45.

Armington, P. S. "A Theory of Demand for Products Distinguished by Place of Production." *IMF Staff Papers* 16 (1969): 159–78.

Baldwin, Robert E. "Are Economists' Traditional Trade Policy Views Still Valid?" *Journal of Economic Literature* 30 (June 1992): 804–29.

Beghin, John C., and Daniel A. Sumner. "Content Requirement and Bilateral Monopoly." *Oxford Economic Papers* 44 (1993): 306–16.

Benedict, Murray R., and Oscar Stine. *The Agricultural Commodity Programs: Two Decades of Experience.* New York: Twentieth Century Fund, 1956.

Blandford, D. "Market Share Models and the Elasticity of Demand for U.S. Agricultural Exports." Chapter 7 in

Elasticities in International Agricultural Trade, edited by C. A. Carter and W. H. Gardiner. Boulder, Colo.: Westview Press, 1988.

Bredahl, M. E., W. Meyers, and K. J. Collins. "The Elasticity of Foreign Demand for U.S. Agriculture Products: The Importance of the Price Transmission Elasticity." *American Journal of Agricultural Economics* 61 (1979): 58–62.

Burt, O. R., and V. E. Worthington. "Wheat Acreage Supply Response in the United States." *Western Journal of Agricultural Economics* 13 (1991): 100–11.

Collins, K. J. "Statement of Keith Collins, Acting Assistant Secretary for Economics, U.S. Department of Agriculture, before the U.S. International Trade Commission, Investigation 22-54 (Wheat, Wheat Flour and Semolina), April 28, 1994." In *Transcript of Proceedings before the United States International Trade Commission*. Washington D.C.: Capitol Hill Reporting, April 28, 1994), pp. 45–63.

Devadoss, S., and W. H. Meyers. "Variability in Wheat Export Demand Elasticity: Policy Implications." *Agricultural Economics* 4 (1990): 381–94.

Dutton, J. "Targeted Export Subsidies as an Exercise of Monopoly Power." *Canadian Journal of Economics* 23 (1990): 705–10.

Dwyer, Michael J. "Effectiveness of MPP in Promoting U.S. High Value Agricultural Exports." Presentation at the annual meeting of the International Agricultural Trade Research Consortium, Washington, D.C., December 16, 1994.

Espy, Mike, and Alice M. Rivlin. Letter to Honorable E. (Kika) de la Garza, chairman, Committee on Agriculture, U.S. House of Representatives. U.S. Department of Agriculture and Office of Management and Budget, September 30, 1994.

Fullerton, D. "Reconciling Recent Estimates of the Marginal Welfare Cost of Taxation." *American Economic Review* 81 (March 1991): 302–8.

Gardiner, W. H., and C. A. Carter. "Issues Associated with Elasticities in International Agricultural Trade." Chapter 1 in *Elasticities in International Agricultural Trade*, edited by C. A. Carter and W. H. Gardiner. Boulder, Colo.: Westview Press, 1988.

Gardner, B. L. "Efficient Redistribution through Commodity Markets." *American Journal of Agricultural Economics* 65 (May 1983): 225–34.

———. "The Political Economy of U.S. Export Subsidies for Wheat." Working Paper 93-06, Department of Agricultural and Resource Economics, University of Maryland, 1993. (Prepared for the National Bureau of Economic Research conference, February 3–4, 1994, Cambridge, Mass.).

de Gorter, H., and K. D. Meilke. "The EEC's Wheat Price Policies and International Trade in Differentiated Products." *American Journal of Agricultural Economics* 69 (1987): 223–29.

Grennes, T., P. R. Johnson, and M. Thursby. *The Economics of World Grain Trade*. New York: Praeger Publishers, 1978.

Hafi, Ahmed, Peter Connell, and Ivan Roberts. "U.S. Sugar Policies." *Australian Commodities* 1 (December 1994): 484–500.

Haley, Stephen L. "U.S. Imports of Canadian Wheat: Estimating the Effects of the U.S. Export Enhancement Program." Economic Research Service, U.S. Department of Agriculture, November, 1994.

Houck, James P. *Elements of Agricultural Trade Policies*. Macmillan Publishing Company: New York, 1986.

International Agricultural Trade Research Consortium. "Bringing Agriculture into the GATT: Potential Use of an Aggregate Measure of Support." Commissioned paper 5, University of Missouri, 1990.

———. *The Uruguay Round Agreement on Agriculture: An Evaluation of the Outcome of the Negotiations.* Commissioned paper 9, Stanford University, 1994.

Johnson, D. Gale. *Trade and Agriculture: A Study of Inconsistent Policies.* New York: John Wiley & Sons, 1950.

———. *The Sugar Program: Large Costs and Small Benefits.*

Evaluative Studies 14. Washington: American Enterprise Institute, 1974.

———. "World Agriculture, Commodity Policy and Price Variability." *American Journal of Agricultural Economics* 57 (1975): 823–28.

———. *World Agriculture in Disarray*. 2d ed. London: Macmillan, 1991.

Josling, Tim, and Stephan Tangermann. "The Significance of Tariffication in the Uruguay Round Agreement on Agriculture." North American Agricultural Policy Research Consortium Workshop, Vancouver, May 14, 1994.

Krishna, Kala, and Marie C. Thursby. "Trade Policy with Imperfect Competition: A Selective Survey." In *Imperfect Competition and Political Economy*, edited by Colin A. Carter and Alex F. McCalla. Boulder, Colo.: Westview Press, 1990.

Krugman, Paul R. "Is Free Trade Passé?" *Journal of Economic Perspectives* 1 (Fall 1987): 131–44.

———. *Peddling Prosperity*. New York: W. W. Norton, 1994.

McCalla, Alex F. "Agricultural Trade Liberalization: The Ever-Elusive Grail." *American Journal of Agricultural Economics* 75 (December 1993): 1102–12.

Orden, David. "Agricultural Interest Groups and the North American Free Trade Agreement." National Bureau of Economic Research, Working Paper 4790, July 1994.

Organization for Economic Cooperation and Development. *Agricultural Policies, Markets and Trade. Monitoring and Outlook, 1990*. Paris, 1991.

Rossen, C. Parr III, C. Ford Runge, and Dale E. Hathaway. "International Trade Agreements." In *Food, Agriculture and Rural Policy into the Twenty-first Century: Issues and Tradeoffs*, edited by Milton Hallberg et al. Boulder, Colo.: Westview Press, 1994, pp. 187–98.

Rucker, Randal R., Walter N. Thurman, and Robert B. Borges. "The Effects of the GATT on U.S. Peanut Markets." In *Supply Management in Transition toward the Twenty-first Century*. Boulder, Colo.: Westview Press, forthcoming.

Salathe, L. "Export Responsiveness and U.S. Farm Policy

Options for Wheat." *Journal of Agricultural Economics Research* 40 (1988): 19–20.

Sanderson, Fred H. "The GATT Agreement on Agriculture." National Center for Food and Agricultural Policy. No date.

Smith, Mark E., and David R. Lee. "Overseas Food Aid Programs." In *Food, Agriculture and Rural Policy into the Twenty-first Century: Issues and Tradeoffs,* edited by Milton Hallberg et al. Boulder, Colo.: Westview Press, 1994, pp. 153–66.

Sumner, Daniel A. "Tobacco and the Uruguay Round." In *Current Issues in Tobacco Economics,* edited by Farrell Delman, Thomas Slane, and Michael Marion. Vol. 4. Princeton, N.J.: Tobacco Merchant Association, 1991, pp. 188–94.

———. "The Economic Underpinnings of Uruguay Round Proposals." In *Improving Agricultural Trade Performance under the GATT,* edited by Tilman Becker, Richard Gray, and Andrew Schmitz. Kiel: Wissenschaftsverlag, Vauk, 1992, pp. 239–50.

———. "Economic Analysis for Better Agricultural Trade Policy." James N. Snyder Memorial Lecture, Department of Agricultural Economics, Purdue University, West Lafayette, Indiana. 1993.

———. "Agricultural Trade Relations between the United States and the European Community: Recent Events and Current Policy." In *Agricultural Trade Conflicts and the GATT: New Dimensions in U.S.-European Agricultural Trade Relations,* edited by Giovanni Anania et al. Oxford: Westview Press, 1994, pp. 101–20.

———. "Tobacco Supply Management with and without Import Barriers: Examples from Policy in the United States and Australia." In *Supply Management in Transition toward the Twenty-first Century.* Boulder, Colo.: Westview Press, forthcoming.

Sumner, Daniel A., and J. M. Alston. *Effects of the Tobacco Program: An Analysis of Decontrol.* Washington D.C.: American Enterprise Institute, 1986.

————. "Substitutability for Farm Commodities: The Demand for U.S. Tobacco in Cigarette Manufacturing." *American Journal of Agricultural Economics* 69:2 (1987): 258–65.

Sumner, Daniel A., J. M. Alston, and R. S. Gray. "A Quantitative Analysis of the Effects of Wheat Imports on the U.S. Market for Wheat Including the Impact on Deficiency Payments." Report prepared for the Canadian Wheat Board, April 25, 1994.

Thursby, Marie C., and Jerry G. Thursby. "Strategic Trade Theory and Agricultural Markets: An Application to Canadian and U.S. Wheat Exports to Japan." In *Imperfect Competition and Political Economy*, edited by Colin A. Carter and Alex F. McCalla. Oxford: Westview Press, 1990.

Trostle, Ronald G., Karl D. Meilke, and Larry D. Sanders. "U.S. Agricultural Trade Policy." In *Food, Agriculture and Rural Policy into the Twenty-first Century: Issues and Tradeoffs*, edited by Milton Hallberg et al. Boulder, Colo.: Westview Press, 1994, pp. 199–219.

Tyers, R., and K. Anderson. *Disarray in World Food Markets: A Quantitative Assessment*. Cambridge: Cambridge University Press, 1992.

U.S.-Canada Binational Panel Final Report. *The Interpretation of and Canada's Compliance with Article 701.3 with Respect to Durum Wheat Sales*. February 8, 1993.

U.S. Department of Agriculture. Economic Research Service. "Embargoes, Surplus Disposal and U.S Agriculture." Agricultural Economic Report 564. December 1986.

————. Economic Research Service. "GATT and Agriculture: the Concepts of PSEs and CSEs." Miscellaneous Publication 1468, Washington, D.C. 1989.

————. Economic Research Service. "Provisions of the Food, Agriculture, Conservation, and Trade Act of 1990." Information Bulletin 624. June 1991.

————. Office of Economics. "Preliminary Analysis of the Economic Implications of the Dunkel Text for American Agriculture," March 1992.

————. Economic Research Service. "Effects of the North American Free Trade Agreement on U.S. Agricultural Commodities," Economic Analysis Staff, March 1993.

————. Foreign Agriculture Service. "GATT-Uruguay Round Fact Sheets." February 1994 (a).

————. Office of Economics. "Effects of the Uruguay Round Agreement on U.S. Agricultural Commodities," March 1, 1994 (b).

————. Economic Research Service. "Foreign Agricultural Trade of the United States." July/August 1994 (c).

————. Economic Research Service. "Agricultural Outlook." AO-213, November 1994 (d).

————. Economic Research Service. "Agricultural Outlook." AO-218, May 1995 (e).

U.S. General Accounting Office. *International Trade: Effectiveness of the Market Promotion Program Remains Unclear.* GAO/GGD-93-103. June 1993.

————. *Wheat Support: The Impact of Target Prices versus Export Subsidies.* GAO/RCED-94-79. June 1994.

U.S. International Trade Commission. *Transcript of Proceedings before the United States International Trade Commission, Investigation No. 22-54 (Wheat, Wheat Flour and Semolina).* Washington, D.C.: Capitol Hill Reporting, April 28, 1994a.

————. *Wheat, Wheat Flour and Semolina: Investigation No. 22-54.* USITC Publication 2794, July 1994b.

U.S., President's Council of Economic Advisers. *Economic Report of the President.* 1993.

Veeman, M. M. "Hedonic Price Functions for Wheat in the World Market: Implications for Canadian Wheat Export Strategy." *Canadian Journal of Agricultural Economics* 35 (1987): 535–52.

Vercammen, James, and Richard Barichello. "Export Credit and Targeted Export Subsidies: Price Discrimination with and without Arbitrage." Working paper, University of British Columbia, Vancouver, 1994.

Vousden, Neil. *The Economics of Trade Protection.* New York: Cambridge University Press, 1990.

Zaini, Hasyim. "An Analysis of the U.S. Tobacco Domestic Content Regulations." Seminar paper, North Carolina State University, Raleigh, November 1994.

Zaini, Hasyim, John Beghin, and Blake Brown. "Complying or Not with Domestic Content Policies? The Case of the U.S. Cigarette Industry." Working paper, North Carolina State University, Raleigh, August 1994.

Index

About the Author

DANIEL A. SUMNER is the Frank H. Buck, Jr., Professor in the Department of Agricultural Economics at the University of California, Davis. He was the assistant secretary for economics at the U.S. Department of Agriculture, where he was the chief economist in policy formulation and analysis on issues facing agriculture and rural America, from food and farm programs to trade, resources, and rural development. Mr. Sumner was a member of the Board of Directors of the U.S. Commodity Credit Corporation, senior economist at the President's Council of Economic Advisers, deputy assistant secretary of agriculture, and professor in the Division of Economics and Business at North Carolina State University.

Mr. Sumner's academic research in agricultural economics focuses on the consequences of domestic and trade policies for agriculture and the economy. His research has appeared in numerous academic journal articles, books, and technical reports.

He is the series editor for the AEI Studies in Agricultural Policy.

149

The American Enterprise Institute
for Public Policy Research

Founded in 1943, AEI is a nonpartisan, nonprofit, research and educational organization based in Washington, D.C. The Institute sponsors research, conducts seminars and conferences, and publishes books and periodicals.

AEI's research is carried out under three major programs: Economic Policy Studies; Foreign Policy and Defense Studies; and Social and Political Studies. The resident scholars and fellows listed in these pages are part of a network that also includes ninety adjunct scholars at leading universities throughout the United States and in several foreign countries.

The views expressed in AEI publications are those of the authors and do not necessarily reflect the views of the staff, advisory panels, officers, or trustees.

A NOTE ON THE BOOK

*This book was edited by Ann Petty
of the publications staff
of the American Enterprise Institute.
The index was prepared by Robert Elwood.
The text was set in Palatino, a typeface
designed by the twentieth-century Swiss designer
Hermann Zapf. Lisa Roman of the AEI Press
set the type, and Edwards Brothers Incorporated,
of Lillington, North Carolina,
printed and bound the book,
using permanent acid-free paper.*

The AEI Press is the publisher for the American Enterprise Institute
for Public Policy Research, 1150 Seventeenth Street, N.W., Washington, D.C. 20036; *Christopher DeMuth*, publisher; *Dana Lane*, director;
Ann Petty, editor; *Leigh Tripoli*, editor; *Cheryl Weissman*, editor; *Lisa
Roman*, editorial assistant (rights and permissions).